MW01126998

Increasing Church Capacity Primer

Learn to Think in Systems

Dr. Steve Smith

Copyright © 2014 ChurchEquippers

All rights reserved. No part of this publication may be reproduced, stored in a retrieval system, or transmitted in any form or by any means, electronic, mechanical, photocopy, recording, or any other—except for brief quotations in printed reviews, without prior permission of the author.

www.ChurchEquippers.com

ISBN: 978-1-941000-03-8

Cover by Brandon Mead

Sola Gloria Deo.

Dedicated to the hard working pastors on the frontlines.

I have learned so much from you.

Table of Contents

INTRODUCTION

I met a great church planter in a restaurant. He was a sharp, articulate entrepreneur kind of guy, just at the front end of what will probably be a very long and fruitful ministry. Since successfully planting his church four years before, he had started two other daughter churches in nearby towns. As he shared the details of these different churches, he mentioned that one was running over 1000 people. I had already learned that he was still seeking to break the 200 barrier for his church so it could grow further. Intrigued, I asked him why one of his daughter churches had grown so much bigger and faster than the one which had initiated it. He answered without hesitation, "When that pastor started, he had a partner who was all about systems. That's all this guy does—put together the systems that make the church work. I, on the other hand, do not understand systems and need to learn."

That planter's experience is why I teach healthy church systems to both church planters and pastors of established churches. I know that systems alone are not the magic pill leaders are looking for in order to grow a church. But I also know that even terrific leaders cannot increasingly win, disciple, retain, train and guide new people into the life of the faith community without workable systems. It does not matter how spiritually deep your walk is with God, how outstanding your preaching is, or even how good an evangelist you are. The church is an organism that requires functional structures to grow. To ignore systems is to put an unseen lid on your growth capacity.

I have been a systems coach for over a decade. I have mentored pastors who took systems seriously. One of the first planters I coached in systems came up with a visual model for his systems based on building a house from the foundation up. His church continues to grow.

Another pastor realized he would not be the one who developed the systems for his church, so he brought the leader who *would* to our coaching sessions. He still thanks me every time I see him and has referred a number of church planters to me for help. I also have sat with those who listened politely, took no notes, did none of the challenging work, and continue to wonder why their church does not grow.

You might wonder why systems coaching is necessary. After all, church structure and processes seem pretty simple, even familiar. I was in that camp when I was a pastor and had to learn the hard way that I did not know what I did not know about systems. Today I repeat this little slogan often when answering the 'why' question: *If they already knew how to do it, they'd be doing it.* Pastors who have already mastered these things do not need me to tell them what they already know. What I have also learned through the years is that pastors are 'new information' addicts. We are like advanced Trivial Pursuit players, collecting more facts and figures to toss out when talking shop with other pastors or when we need to impress leaders with our acumen. But here is the difference between a pastor of a growing church and one whose church is not—the first pastor has pursued mastery over knowledge. Mastery is the difference between a weekend hacker and a PGA contender. Between singing in the shower and winning an American Idol contest. Those who want to make and retain new disciples understand that they cannot just be conversant in systems; they have to know how systems work and interact so they can guide their congregation in building the right systems for their church.

If your church is not growing, if your church has a bigger back door than front door, if you have watched your congregation turnover while you have been at the church you lead, or if you are at the frontend of starting a new church, then you are the one that I am encouraging to explore this primer. There are some things you do not know. Understand that this is an introduction to what you need to know about systems. You will need more than this primer to move your church from beginner to mastery. And you will probably discover along the way that you will need at least a staff partner, if not a team, to build the kind of systems that will grow your church. Many pastors are big picture people, seeing the church in terms of the hoped for goals, but are not the detail people who can build of the systems to get there. A strong majority of these pastors lean towards seeing their churches in terms of what I call the golden triangle—numbers of people at the weekly gathering, totals for the weekly giving and building size. These three talking points for many pastoral gatherings create a myopic focus away from the rest of the essential systems that make the church healthy.

Systems coaching cuts across all the various approaches to how you construct your church's life. Regardless of your church's size, style, denomination or age, it has the same eighteen systems that every other church on your block has. Are you leading an attractional model church? A theologically driven model church? A traditional model church? No approach works any better than any other model without systems. If you are convinced that it's style over substance that causes growth you're going to be disappointed over and over again. You are deceiving yourself and possibly missing out on what you really want—a growing church.

Five reasons why you should work on your church's systems:

1) Your church will become healthier. Having broken or incomplete systems is like missing an arm or a lung. You can get by, but it is harder and you are less effective.

2) Your church will begin to reproduce. If you are intent on cooperating with God in expanding His Kingdom's reach in your community, you will need to reproduce disciples, leaders, ministries and new churches. This takes healthy working systems.

3) You as the pastor will be able to focus your energies. Instead of spending time trying to fill the gaps caused by broken or incomplete systems, healthy systems allow others to offer appropriate leadership, freeing you to do what God has called you to do.

4) Your congregation will be able to grow and change without losing ground. In a church without healthy systems, the loss of a member can spell the end of a ministry process until someone new shows up. Healthy systems allow for the continued development of people within the congregation to step into the gap left by a past ministry leader or even to expand the ministry to meet the current needs.

5) Your church will increase its capacity to retain the new disciples God is sending you. This is the heart of developing systems. If you want to effectively prepare for a greater harvest of people, you want to strengthen your church's systems.

Let me ask you a question. If I can show you how to not only increase your church's capacity for growth, but to actually grow your church through systems, are you interested? If through systems training you can increase the number of leaders working with you, does that interest you? If your church can see an increased flow of those who are saying 'yes' to Jesus for the first time, begin making disciples who are growing in a transformational faith journey at a steady pace, or adding significant ministries to your church without having to ask leaders to double up on responsibilities, do you want to know how to do it?

I invite you to discover through this introduction what you do not know about healthy systems. You may say you already know how to do this or the other system. But what if you have overlooked something that can make your system stronger and more productive? Your system may not be missing much, but what is missing may be the key difference between growth and frustration. It'll be worth your time to find out and do it better.

SYSTEMS VISUAL

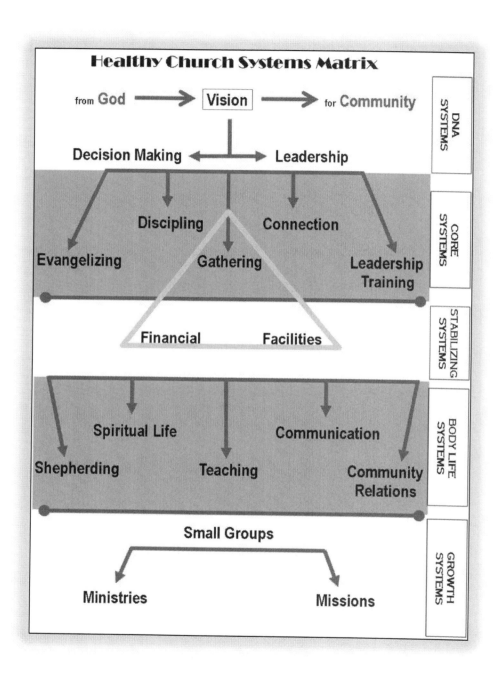

1. WHAT IS A SYSTEM?

System is a word used to define the dynamics of how your church does its ministry in each area. It does not mean program. It is merely a descriptive moniker for *how your church gets important functions done regularly and consistently*. These systems define the culture of your church. Other churches may do the same tasks differently. What you do depends on the Spirit and your church's vision.

When I use the word 'system' many church leaders hear 'program,' but these two words are not synonymous. Programs are really packaged pieces of a system, the parts that can be bundled and marketed to other churches. For example, you see that another church has a highly successful children's ministry program and you find that you can buy it for your church. What you have bought is a ministry idea, a curriculum. What the program does not include is the recruiting, training, resourcing and evaluation processes that make up the rest of the system. Systems are the whole pie, all the working parts necessary to function successfully.

The starting point to system thinking is that there is *no one right or only way to do any church system*. Do not be drawn into believing otherwise by those who might claim that their way is the biblical way. Not that there is anything wrong with copying all or parts of another church's system. The issue is to make sure you choose a way of doing a system for your church that is in keeping with the vision and strategy that you are pursuing. There are ways of constructing a system in your church that will never work for you just because they are not suitable for your situation. Knowing this will save you time and frustration.

For example, suppose you decide that doing Sunday School in the traditional way is better for your congregation than having groups meet in homes during the week. Both of these represent varieties of a small group system. Neither is better nor worse than the other, if you can show that the one you chose works for your congregation. Though I have used both styles as a pastor, meeting in homes is no more biblical than meeting in a building. Those that argue for a biblical model of home based groups from glimpses we get of the earliest church in Acts fail to mention that there were no church buildings to meet in until the fourth century! On the other hand, if church building based groups do not work for your situation, remember that doing it that way is not mandated by God.

Here is the real question for any system you use: Is there evident fruit from the way you do it? If the system you use is not producing the results you are asking it to produce, then either the system is missing some necessary parts or it is not being led by the right leader. Or the problem may be that you have outgrown the system you are using because you have grown to another level of attendance. While this is a good problem, failing to address this in a timely fashion may discourage the people you are trying to serve through that system and throttle your growth potential.

What a system is supposed to do is inherent within itself. Dr. Donella Meadows, in her book, *Thinking in Systems*, talked about her favorite way to introduce this truth. Standing before her class, she would put a Slinky in her hand and grab it by the top. Then she would pull her bottom hand away and the Slinky would unwind down to the floor. She would ask the students why the Slinky slinked. Most often, people would say it was because she had removed her hand. Challenging that notion, she would then pick up the box the Slinky came in, place it on her hand and also grasp it by the top. When her lower hand was then removed with a flourish, the box just stayed boxed—no slinking to the floor. Her point? Just as the Slinky bounced up and down because that is what Slinkys do and the box stayed boxed because it was made to be a box, so every system behaves consistently with its internal structure.

Apply this to your systems. Does your discipling system produce the transforming disciples you expect it to? Does your evangelizing system regularly lead people to saying 'yes' to Jesus? Are people more aware of what is happening in your church because your communication system brings about better listening? If one of your church's systems is not producing what you thought it should produce, it is because of how it is put together and not because of something from outside of it working to defeat it.

You need to accept that *outside forces rarely have any influence on systems' internal effectiveness* or you will be playing the blame game instead of addressing the right issues. For example, think about conversion growth and a church's evangelizing system. All of the research on the percentage of lost people in America suggests that almost all churches are surrounded by more people who do not follow Jesus than all the church buildings in their community can hold. Yet it is common to hear the complaint that a nearby church plant or a neighboring mega-church is the reason our church is not growing. Everyone is now going to the place where there are new bells and whistles. But what is *really* true is that your church's evangelizing system is not working because something is wrong *within* it, not because these other churches are reaching every possible lost person in the neighborhood. *If you cannot accept this, learning about systems will be of no value to you.*

This points to something else about church systems. Systems do not work individually. They work only in harmony with the other systems. Perhaps the church does not evangelize well because it doesn't have a good evangelizing system. But the evangelizing system does not stand alone. The church has other systems that should be interacting with the evangelizing system that may not be doing what they were made to do either.

"Why is my church not growing?" is a common question people who are exploring systems ask. The answer does vary. In the previous illustration, the evangelizing system was the problem. But I have seen churches that have people regularly say 'yes' to Jesus and still not grow. For some, their discipling system did not move new believers past babyhood faith and they became discouraged and left. Others lacked good connection systems, so new believers felt like outsiders and eventually dropped out. Or the church lacked a robust shepherding system and these people did not get their needs met consistently, so they wandered away in time. Or it was a combination of all of these system problems. Healthy growing churches depend on their systems working together because the church itself is systemic in nature.

You may object to that characterization. The idea of systems to many people suggests organization, which some think is a bad thing. Is Jesus' church an organization or an organism? Which is it? In my lifetime, the idea that the church is an organism, not an organization, has been advanced and argued vigorously. Proponents have pointed to the biblical idea that the church is the *body of Christ* as proof of their position. To them, the idea that the church is an organization negatively points towards being a social group that has officers, rules and policies. This, they argue, has more to do with a group like the Elks or Shriners than being Jesus' visible body. The descriptive word they prefer for the church is "organic." And being the organic church is far more desirable than carrying the label, "organized religion."

Except this is all artificial. Yes, a number of churches exist that are more about being social groups than being a witness of the gospel to their community. Certainly quite a few churches are more about positions, procedures and prominence than proclamation. But these aberrations are not the definitive meaning of "organization."

Science has shown us that the simple cell of any organism is really incredibly complex. Within every cell are systems for transport, respiration, synthesis, assimilation, growth, excretion, regulation, reproduction, and metabolism—all crammed into an extremely small package. The cell is the ultimate organized organism.

If you speak of your church as being a body, then you also have to acknowledge that all bodies have multiple functioning systems which keep them alive. The human body has muscular, circulatory, digestive, excretory, neurological, skeletal and reproductive systems, among others, working symbiotically. This is the way God made us. As we grow physically, our interlocking systems are supposed to grow with us. This is also true for the organic church body. The healthy church is an organism that has interacting systems. It is an organized organism. Leaders who understand this and value systems will be ready to position their church to *increase its capacity for growth.*

Are church systems ungodly or unspiritual? I sometimes get pushback about this. When I coach systems with some leadership teams, the response I get is that systems are not biblical. Or maybe they are not spiritual. A leader once retorted that the church is depending on the Holy Spirit for its growth needs, implying that systems were to be checked at the door along with other worldly ideas. And yet, when the apostles were challenged with the possible neglected needs of the Greek-speaking widows of the Jerusalem congregation in Acts 6, what did the apostles do? They initiated a system that they borrowed from the synagogues. They asked the congregation to appoint seven men, who are considered to have been the first deacons, to take ongoing care of the issue. Later Paul and Barnabas would appoint both elders and deacons to the churches they started on their first missionary journey. Why? Because the deacon system fed the life of the congregation.

Here is the difference between the church as an organization and the church as an organized organism. The life of the congregation is truly from the Spirit, not systems. But churches, like all organisms, have life sustaining systems that need to be nurtured or the church will be weaker and smaller than it needs to be.

If you look closely at any church, you will discern that each has eighteen different systems. They may not share the same outward features, but structurally, they function to accomplish exactly the same things (or not, if the system is broken). These systems can be grouped into five categories. (see diagram on page 1)

DNA systems: They are the foundational systems of any church. These three systems define the future direction and strategies that will guide this church. The *vision* is the bedrock upon which all the other systems will be built. The *leadership* of the church has to be in agenda harmony with this vision. Agenda harmony clears the way for collaborative *decision-making* so that leaders can move forward together.

Core systems: These five systems—*evangelizing, discipling, gathering, connections* and *leadership training*—provide the lifeblood of the church. These systems are core because they define the primary work of the leaders in developing a congregation. Making disciples who pursue intimacy with God is the principal function of Christ's church. How people come to faith, grow in that faith and become part of the congregation, as well as begin participating in its mission is defined by these systems.

Stabilizing systems: Two systems—*finances* and *facilities*—make it possible for a congregation to become established in a community. Every church body has to have a home, even if it is using rented facilities or some public area. All churches handle money for some reason, either for its operational costs, for missions, for paying God's servants or a combination of all of these. These systems help the church stabilize its place in its community and maintain its ongoing presence.

Body Life systems: All congregations have their own way of pursuing intimacy with God together. These five systems—*shepherding, spiritual life, teaching,* *communication* and *community relationship*—tie the people of the congregation together with God, each other and the community in which they live and have been called to sow and water the gospel.

Growth systems: If you have been around churches for any length of time, you know how people come in the front door and go out the back door of the church. It takes more than a good worship gathering to hold onto people who attend. People connect deeply to a church through its *small groups, ministries* and *missions.* These systems fuel the ongoing growth of a church body.

There is something else you need to know about the above categories. An unbalanced emphasis on certain systems can define your church in unhealthy ways. Churches that burn out people focus most of their attention on the *core systems.* All focus is on bringing people in, with a lack of focused attention given to the personal needs of those who are already in. On the flip side, plateaued churches emphasize the *body life systems.* They are all about caring for people inside the group and give only lip service to expecting people to engage in making new disciples and leaders. Growing churches make sure both of these two groups of systems are functioning at a high level. People need the challenge of the core systems to sow, water and reap the gospel in the community. But they also need to be shepherded. Do not value certain kinds of systems over others. They all matter.

Churches need every one of these systems to be healthy and working together to accomplish their mission. If one system is not healthy, the whole church is adversely affected. If many systems are off-line, the church is in crisis. The crisis can be ignored for some time if the church is happily reaping the benefit of its healthier systems. But because systems function symbiotically—each one feeding the others—the church will continue to lose people it might have retained. This leakage will have nothing to do with the friendliness of the church, its spiritual temperature or doctrinal integrity. The loss will be due to not being an organized organism.

2. INCREASING CAPACITY

The church I was visiting had grown from a plant to over 1000 attenders. I sat with the pastor before the Sunday morning celebration and listened to him express both the blessing and challenge of leading such a large congregation. As I probed his current needs, he suddenly said, "I need help. I find that the systems that worked well when the church was at 250 people are no longer doing the job for us now." What he meant was the systems that had been set up to handle 250 people lacked the capacity for 1000 and were now overtaxed and workers were being burned out. People who were looking for ways to connect more deeply with the church were finding "no vacancy" signs on the doors of the growth systems—small groups, ministries and missions—that formerly had absorbed all who tried to enter in the past. After months of frustration, they would wander away to another congregation.

Maybe you have had a similar experience with people who explored joining your church family. You feel like you are a good pastor and that your congregation is pretty healthy. Maybe you are averaging 60 or 120 or 200 in attendance right now and believe the current influx of visitors could strengthen your church's impact on the community. But it just appears that people who would have stayed and become part of the congregation—maybe they attended for numerous months—started attending another congregation without a reasonable cause. I suggest that a possible reason is that your church has systems that prevent the congregation from retaining people. In short, *you lack capacity for more people.*

Churches face growth barriers when they add people through conversion and transfer growth. Barriers are not just about where you find more people to lead and shepherd. Barriers exist when you fill up all the slots that can comfortably be filled in a system. If your systems can take care of forty people, the forty-first will spill out. The hypothetical question, "What would you do if God sent one hundred new people to your church today?" is answered by most churches with the probable answer, "Lose them." Why? Because for most churches, their systems will just not absorb more people.

It is probable that you have never grasped that this is a valid reason explaining why certain churches grow and others do not. As you think about your church, you may not have a clue about the systems with which you have an increasing capacity issue. You may even feel defensive about the way you "do church." If I asked, you would probably point to all kinds of reasons people should have stayed—your theological depth, your commitment to the family, or even the classic, "We are a friendly church!" You like your church family and its ways of getting things done. If those visitors had stayed, they would have discovered that your church is a fun place to be.

Let me clue you in—what is fun and functional at one growth level may keep you from going on to the next. Children are fun when they are toddlers. But you would be concerned if your teenager had the skeletal make-up or the brain capacity of a two year old. You should have the same level of concern if you want your church to grow. The systems that you develop and use have to match the needs of your congregation's growth into its next stage of life. *Church systems must grow and change* to allow the church to grow. This is the decisive issue. Upgrading a variety of systems in your church is critical for overcoming each progressive growth barrier.

Increasing a church's size also means becoming a different kind of organized organism. Do not misunderstand the implications of this truth. Every time a church grows to another level in size, the speed of the leaders' decisions and the pressure on systems increases. Think of this in terms of baseball. When a child plays in little league, he or she is doing the same things a pro baseball player is. The child fields, throws and bats, just like a big leaguer. But a child, even a teen, could not hit a fastball thrown by a professional pitcher. Or run the bases at the speed needed to beat the throw of a pro outfielder. Church size has this same aspect. To lead and maintain the next size up church, the pastor and leaders have to gain skills at being a team as well as increase their speed in diagnosing problems, shifting system approaches and implementing changes.

Leading a growing church means figuring out how to do differently from the way it has been done up to now what is needed to be a healthy and spiritually alive congregation. Otherwise, the lack of attention to capacity-increasing systems will not only limit growth, it can reverse growth. Not having the appropriate systems to consolidate new growth can also burn out staff and ministers trying to meet all the emerging needs.

Before discussing what systems you may need to upgrade in order to increase capacity at your church, it is helpful to categorize church sizes. Different studies have offered diverse groupings, so the one offered here is only a guideline to help you determine where your church is currently. In each category of the kind of church mentioned, the median range of attendance is **bolded.**

2-**35-50**—A **family church** where everyone is still able to meet in a house together. This kind of church tends to be tightly knit and have people involved in all decisions. Often the pastor is bi-vocational at this size.

51-**110-150**—A **single-cell church** in which the pastor partners with a changeable lay team to offer leadership. Connection to this church for new people is often through the pastor, who functions as a shepherd.

151-**250**-350—A **multi-celled church**, in which people may not know all the attenders by name. The leadership is often given by a select group of people who work with the pastor. Connection in this church is through its small groups. The pastor functions as an equipper.

351-**600**-900—A **large church**, which is led by a combination of staff ministry leaders and a lay eldership (called by various names). Connection with this church is through a variety of Growth Systems (Small Groups, Ministries, Missions). The pastor functions as a leader over leaders.

901-**2000**-plus—A **decentralized church**, which is staff-led. Connection to this church is self-determined and new people often attach themselves according to their needs or interests apart from the church well defined growth systems. The pastor functions as the primary vision-caster.

Each size church has unique challenges which call for a different way to do its systems. If you are seeking to grow to the next size, then you will not want to set up your church's systems to fit the size you are now but where you plan to go. Otherwise you are not increasing capacity and will bounce up and then back down to the level you are now.

I am watching a church grow again as it intentionally sows the gospel into the community. The leaders have targeted lost people, inviting them to events designed to build relationships and verbalize the good news. People are responding and dozens have made faith decisions and been baptized. The pastor told me that he is facing a systems crisis. Their meeting room is running out of space and they do not have the capacity at this moment to disciple all the people who have been saved. They are now on a fast track towards addressing these logjams and increasing their capacity.

What Systems Need Attention to Increase Capacity?

Beyond these questions, in order to develop increased capacity, first become familiar with the features of the system you need to develop. Then visit churches the next size up to see how their system is put together and functions for their level. Note that you are to seek the next size up instead of churches several levels away. Do not make the common mistake of seeking to do what the decentralized churches do when you are so much smaller than they. Your church is not ready for such a leap and you will be discouraged when you fail to get the results you were hoping for. Your plan of action is to develop a system which your church could and should do now.

Understand that when you are seeking to increase capacity, you are always managing tension. Not the tension of *having* more people—the tension of not being *ready* for more people. More people always stress systems. You will find that you never have enough leaders, resources or space for your systems to absorb the new people you are reaching. You have to accept this and learn to 'ride the curve.' You will probably always be behind the readiness curve, but if you pay attention to your systems and have the right leaders in place, you will see that your systems are capable of flexing and growing even in the midst of the tension.

To grow a church, all systems will need to be revisited and tweaked for every level. But at each level, you have to know which systems are the critical ones to address in order to avoid bottlenecks. And system adjustments are not the only issue. For a pastor to lead his congregation in modifying systems, he must also retool his outlook on his role. Here is an overview of what is critical to address at each level.

Going from a family church (35) to a single-cell church (125)

Decision-making: The pastor must move away from group decision-making to leadership decision-making in some form.

Evangelizing: The attenders must embrace their role in making the church evangelistically effective.

Discipling: There must be a definite process for taking new Christians and growing them into co-workers.

Connection: A family church tends to be clannish and exclusive. The pastor must teach them to recognize and change this pattern.

Gathering: The congregation must develop a gathering system that is inclusive rather than "just for us."

Financial: The congregation must be invested in its future to afford a larger space. Greater accountability with the finances is required for this step.

Facility: The congregation must have room to grow. To go to the 125 level, space is needed to seat 120 adults and teens plus a room or rooms for children.

Pastoral mindset: The pastor must assume the role of equipper. A bottleneck occurs when he is the only one doing what the church is supposed to be doing. He must stop doing the work of the congregation for them and train people to evangelize and disciple. He also must make time to connect with new attenders.

Going from a single-cell church to a multi-cell church (250)

Leadership Training: The pastor must develop a training process for emerging leaders and invest heavily in time with them.

Connection: The pastor must move from allowing everyone to connect relationally with him to a connection system that utilizes other people, groups and ministries.

Shepherding: A system of shepherding care must be offered through lay leaders in the congregation rather than wholly by the pastor alone.

Small groups: The church must develop a healthy small group system to help create relational connections among its other functions.

Facility: The congregation must have room to grow. To go to the 250 level, space is needed to seat 220 adults and teens plus rooms for children. This can be accomplished by going to two services if you have room for 120 in your main room.

Pastoral mindset: He must learn the art of delegation, rolling off critical responsibilities to newly raised up leaders regardless of his attachment to those duties. A bottleneck is created when the pastor is trying to be everything to every attender.

Going from a multi-celled church (250) to a large church (500)

Communications: At this size, many things are happening every week and people need to know what is important for them and what is optional. A good communication system will help people still feel connected in spite of the congregation's size.

Ministries: The church must weigh the ministries it has in order to see if they are helping to increase the capacity.

Mission: The church must start planting the next church if it has not already. This counter-intuitive step will actually drive growth.

Facility: The congregation must have room to grow. To go to the 500 level, space is needed to seat 480 adults and teens plus a room or rooms for children, or go to multiple services. The congregation also needs places to meet and connect apart from the main gathering.

Pastoral mindset: He must focus on leading leaders and not be threatened by having strong leaders around him. A bottleneck happens when he surrounds himself with leaders who are weaker than he is. They will hesitate to take initiative when they need to because they are waiting for him to give them permission.

Going from a large church (500) to a decentralized church (1000+)

Decision Making: Because of the increased speed and broader scope of decision making, the church must shift from lay leader decision making to staff decision making.

Leadership: The church must have staff members who develop others instead of being specialists who personally lead ministry. The church will also need to build up more leaders.

Gathering: The church must begin to diversify its gathering style to speak to the heart language of different groups of people it is seeking to reach.

Ministries: The church must increase its ministries to meet the challenge of the increasing diversity of people.

Mission: The church must become more engaged in mission to its Jerusalem if it is deficient in this.

Facility: The congregation must have room to grow. To go to the 1000 level, space is needed to seat 450 adults and teens with multiple services or a room that holds 900 people. Larger children's spaces will be needed.

Pastoral Mindset: He must develop multiple partner leaders and be willing to share his pulpit with other speakers to free up his time to lead growth in the church. He will need to focus his time on what he alone can do and have leaders around him who lead in their strengths.

Growing as a decentralized church (1000+)

Leadership: You must double your leadership from the last level and keep doubling it.

Decision Making: The church must be staff-led instead of lay-led.

Connection: The church must utilize visible people and communication to help people learn how to connect deeply with the congregation. This system will call for multiple connection points in small groups, ministries and missions.

Shepherding: Because of the amount of people, this system must be able to guide people towards ways of getting their needs attended to who do not become part of a small group or ministry team.

Facility: The congregation must have room to grow. To go beyond the 1000+ level, space is needed to seat 600 adults and teens with multiple services or a worship facility that is specific to the emerging needs.

Pastoral Mindset: He will need higher spiritual accountability than ever in his ministry. Failure to take this seriously could result in blowing up the ministry through personal moral failure or pride. Remember, in Jesus' Kingdom, no church is too big to fail. I watched a church of 5000 disappear out of a community due to the pastor's failure as a leader and as God's man over a period of 15 years. Do not let this be said of you.

At each level, the lead pastor has to list duties and decide which are his core responsibilities and which have to be done by others for the church to grow. A pastor has to continually 'reinvent' himself, i.e. gain more and better skills in his ministry to lead the church in growth and outreach.

Conclusion

Increasing capacity takes focus on your systems. Sure, growth can just happen. God orchestrates the growth of His church. You probably know of a church that blew right through a growth stage and kept moving on to the next. But if you take the time to look closely, you will find a pastor and his team that either already knew how to modify their church systems to retain the growth or they were blessed with a coach and were quick learners.

As you read through the systems later in the primer, think about what size your church falls into at this time. What systems would you need to learn to adjust to increase your capacity? Consider the following strategy to accelerate your learning curve. Find one or more solid churches that are at the next level of growth from you. Meet with the pastors and find out how they do particular systems that you need to understand and which changes they made and when they made them. Unless you are a step away from becoming a decentralized church, do not look at their systems for guidance. Why? Because their systems are fueled by far more resources than you have at the moment. The church that has successfully grown the next size up from yours will be able to give you workable ideas that may work in your situation as well.

3. THREE BOTTLENECKS TO INCREASING CAPACITY

What does it mean for a church to increase capacity? It means discovering and getting past current bottlenecks that keep you from growing. More positively it means determining how to develop a system for the next stage of growth. Growth is not a dirty word. It is the natural outcome of a church which sows the gospel intentionally into the community around it. It is never the goal of the church to grow. Growth should be the outcome of the church being whole and healthy. I'll address that idea later.

Three questions can help you evaluate your church's current systems' capacity.

1. Has this system continued to grow and absorb the incoming people we are ministering to? Or is it maxed out and showing a tendency to plateau?

For example, if your evangelizing system has produced 10 to 15 conversions a year for multiple years, your system is probably plugged up. But you may have never questioned its serviceability because 10-15 felt like enough for you. What if you could, by making changes in your evangelizing system, increase your capacity and see a greater harvest? Or perhaps your discipling system maxes out at 40 people going through it at any one time when you really need it to handle 60. Or maybe your leadership training system is productive, but only produces enough replacement leaders to maintain your current ministries. What this indicates is the systems you have will not stretch far enough to help the church do more. They may not even adequately cover the needs of the current attenders even if you did not grow.

The search for an increased capacity system starts with the realization that one or more of the systems you have cannot grow any larger. If your desire is to hold on to all the potential attenders coming through your church's doors, it does not help if your connection system is already maxed out and will not allow you to incorporate this influx of new people into the life of the church—or your communication system leaves lots of people in the dark about what's going on.

This leads to the issue of the *Too Many/Too Few Rule* for evaluating capacity for a system. This rule is that if you have too many people who are not being served by the system you have and are burning out the too few people serving the system, you are already late in changing what you are doing to increase capacity. For example, if your discipling system is designed to do one-on-one discipleship for 25 people a year, then the day you have 26 people, you have both too many people in need and too few servers available. Asking busy people to double up on discipling will only result in burnout. You are left with two choices, to add more disciplers or change your system to do cohort discipling. Or say you are adding 1-2 new small groups a year, but to connect all the new people who are exploring a relationship with the church, you need five new groups every six months. You can either accept that you are going to see 80-100 people not connect deeply with your congregation and probably lose them out the back door, or you can determine instead to change your way of doing small groups from the one that is proving too constrictive.

Having too few people to run a system has to be addressed proactively. The danger of not doing so is that the servers will be forced to take on more responsibilities—doubling up—as the capacity limit is passed. The old adage that 20% of the attenders do 80% of the work in the church is the snapshot of this rule. Instead of asking people to do more because the church now has more attenders to service, the *Too Many/Too Few Rule* should prompt you to notice that your system no longer works effectively. And to see that you may be hurting the workers you have.

The challenge of the *Too Many/Too Few Rule* is that it reveals one of the fundamental flaws in church systems. Many of the ways churches decide to do a system cannot later be expanded to allow a church to grow. But the church becomes comfortable with doing things its own way, even enjoying and bragging on their particular approach of doing a system. Why? Because when it was developed, it was very effective. So even though it is not now as effective, the church has become enamored and even protective of doing the system their way.

If the *Too Many/Too Few Rule* is left unaddressed, you will either lose people out the door or the congregation will remain underdeveloped. What you need to do is when you see that one of your systems is approaching a 90% full level, it is time to consider what other ways that system can be restructured to allow your church to continue to grow. (This does not apply to meeting space, which hits full capacity at 80%.) You calculate the percentage of the *too many* by dividing the people the system is serving by the number of people it was meant to serve. You determine the *too few* servers in two ways. The first is calculating how many servers you need for the current system to work versus how many you actually have. This is a simple "counting the cost" approach where you determine, for example, that if a system needs ten people to operate successfully, is the church trying to get by with less? Or if you need to increase the capacity of that system, how many more people would it need?

The second approach is tabulating the number of hours your servers are putting in. You discover this by surveying the servers themselves. Some servers will have greater time availability. But when 50% or more of the servers are giving over 4 hours a week to run the system, including prep time at home (this is apart from participation in the body life of the church), they are generally maxed out and will begin to burn out if the system remains unchanged.

Just so you know—burnout does not have to be the "end game" option. The "Too Few" side of the rule is not inflexible. It is possible to use the same amount of

26

people you already have in a system if you change the system's basic approach. For example, perhaps your church has a small group system that involves 12-15 people meeting in homes during the week. At the 250 level, you would need potentially 20 groups of this size just to service the current attenders. To develop a system that would allow you to grow to the 500 level, you might choose to change your small group system to mini-congregations with 30-40 members overseen by leaders trained to be lay pastors. You could run this system with the same 20 leaders once they were trained under this new approach.

2. Which systems are being starved because of another system's failure that is nearer the top of the Systems Matrix? This is the *Broken Upline Rule.* Think of the Systems Matrix as flowing from top to bottom. If certain systems at the top of the matrix are neglected, the systems below them will be affected. If you do not have enough small groups (bottom), is it because you do not have enough leaders in development (top)? And if you do not have enough leaders in development, is it because your connection system is not helping you retain potential leaders (top)? Or is it because your discipleship system is not developing enough people to a co-worker level so that they can be trained as leaders (top)? If people are not drawn to serve in your ministry system (bottom), is it because you have failed to connect the vision of the church to those ministries in their thinking (top)? Or has the leadership been so demanding of time and sacrifice that people are unwilling to serve under their regime (top)?

The impact of the broken upline issue is to rob you of the ability to retain and grow more disciples. In turn, the church will probably remain at the size level it is currently. There is a certain level of denial that accompanies this fact. We tend to blame the people we are seeking to retain as being the cause of their departure. "If they had just stayed and helped us start a _____ ministry..." is one common comfort saying we employ. "They are merely church hoppers," is another way we comfort ourselves when the real issue is our failure to examine and correct our broken upline problems. If broken upline systems are not feeding lower systems properly at this level, you will be hard pressed to move on to the next level. Addressing a broken upline problem takes ruthless honesty on your part.

Not having enough leaders for your growth systems is one important aspect of the broken upline problem. To address this issue correctly, you have to think beyond your current need to the next level need. I was in conversation with a pastor who had four small groups and needed four more yesterday. His solution was to begin training four new leaders. My advice was to begin training eight to twelve new leaders, even if some took longer to develop. If he followed his course, he would have created a new broken upline lid to his small group system almost as soon as he finished launching the new groups. *Never think in terms of what you need today, but what you will need when you get what you need today.* If group systems fuel your church's ability to enfold new people deeply into the congregation, you want to continually be able to offer more small groups, ministries and missions to those coming into your gatherings.

Why systems fall apart internally is also a broken upline issue of your leadership system. While you might talk about wanting your church to be a flat organization, leadership systems cannot really be totally flat. A leadership system must have leaders over leaders or every leader will do what is right in their own eyes (this will be covered more in that system module). The point here is that you will create a broken upline problem in your church if you do not intentionally work at developing leaders over leaders to coach, mentor and quality control your various systems.

3. How many systems depend on the pastor to run? This is the *Pastor-Centric Rule*. The more systems that depend on the pastor to operate properly, the more inefficient they are for growth, since the pastor can only accommodate so many people and give so much time before he is maxed out. This is a real capacity limiting issue that is often overlooked because the pastor either likes doing it all or he feels responsible to keep all the systems operating. Many pastors become trapped by this problem because they are trying to fill the system gaps in their church by doing the systems themselves "just for a while" until "someday" when they will have a fix for this system—a someday that does not come.

A clear and pervasive example of this is in the Connection System. Research tells us that 60% plus of churches in America are running 100 people or less. Why? Well, one reason is the church is pastor-centric. By this I mean that, unless we are speaking about a church made up of a single family group, the church is dependent on the pastor to be their all-in-all connector. He is the one they connect with in order to get their needs met. And since the maximum close relationships most pastors can personally maintain is somewhere between 40 to 80 adults, when someone new comes to the church, one of two things happen. Either the newbie will not stay because the pastor has not time for him or her or the newbie will displace someone who has already been there for some time. That displaced person will eventually leave the church, saying their needs are no longer being met. The church will stay on the same attendance plateau with some highs and lows. In short, the pastor is the Connection System. The church will be a single cell one for as long as this is the case. Since many pastors really like being needed as a shepherd, this model suits them even if they are frustrated that the church is not growing.

Addressing pastor-centric tendencies in yourself starts with seeing the truth of what you lead—or don't lead but should. I met with a pastor who was a great speaker and the weekend gathering was meaningful and wholistic. He had been hitting the 150 mark and wanted to go on to the next level, but continued to bounce backwards. So we pulled out the Systems Matrix to do a review of how his systems were doing. Of the five core systems (Evangelizing, Discipling, Gathering, Connection and Leadership Training), he or his wife ran the first four. He had no time to give to the one for which he as pastor was most responsible—Leadership Training. He recognized that until he passed off the other systems to competent leaders, his church would remain stuck in a holding pattern. It was not his skills as a pastor that held the church back from growth. It was his choice of what was his to lead.

This story also points to the solution of the pastor-centric problem. You cannot just hand off systems to others who have not been prepared to take them. Your calling is to equip others to do the work of the ministry. To overcome pastor-centric lids, you have to invest time in training others to do "your" job. In addition, you have to accept that increasing capacity is a team effort, not a personal effort. If you have never cultivated the ability to develop a working team, to trust the strengths of other leaders or have the tendency to recruit leaders who are more like an audience to your leadership than co-workers, make it your goal to learn these skills. Without them, you will continue to be the center of your church as a shepherd, but not as the equipper it also needs.

This story adds one more dimension to the *Pastor-Centric Rule*. You also must ask how many systems are led by the pastor's spouse. This is the hidden side of the issue. The more systems which are kept in the hands of the pastoral couple, the weaker the growth potential of the church. This is a hard truth to face, largely due to the belief that trained pastors and spouses are better equipped to get the work done right. Do not let this siren sing her sweet song in your ear! Your church will never be stronger than when you have raised up leaders to lead systems that before only you could lead.

4. FOUR SYSTEM CAVEATS

1 **Simplicity, rather than complexity, is always the first goal of system creation.** If you read much on leadership, you have come across the acrostic "K.I.S.S." which means "keep it simple stupid." In practice, this means thinking about how one system feeds another. The evangelizing system should feed the discipling system. The discipling system should feed the leadership training system. The leadership training system should supply leaders for the other systems, and so forth. Thinking this way leads to a simple church format rather than a complex church. The more your systems interrelate, the stronger the church is.

Simplicity also means not creating more time commitments to church activities, no matter how good, with which people are expected to fill up their lives. You may ask people to invest some extra time during certain seasons to expand their growth, but healthy church systems should be made to fit into the rhythms of people's lives and are designed to feed each other so that they flow in the life of the church.

2 **Not everything you try will work for you.** Some wonderful system approach in a church you admire might turn out to be a pig's breakfast in your church. That may hurt and be embarrassing, but be okay with it because it happens to a lot of excellent pastors who failed at some church system before they got it right. So if what you tried did not work, do not give up. The system still needs to be developed because it is necessary for the healthy work of your church. Your challenge is to find a workable and healthy way to make this system work for your congregation.

As the leader, your role is to be quick to evaluate why the system is not working and change direction as rapidly as possible. But make sure you are evaluating and not having a knee-jerk reaction. Some systems take time to knit into your church's culture. As Christian Swartz discovered in Natural Church Development, in a healthy church, if a system is operating at a 65% effective rate, it's healthy. And if all the church's systems are at that level, the church will grow. Keep this in mind as you evaluate your systems.

3 **You will not create healthy church systems as a pastor if you are not ready to lead as a pastor.** I know this is a primer about systems. But I cannot ignore the truth that many churches are not so much troubled by the lack of healthy systems are they are by a lack of spiritual health in their pastor. Numerous pastors I worked with were not engaged in a true transformation journey for themselves, hiding unresolved spiritual issues until the issues exploded out of them or the pastor quit the church in frustration, blaming the church for his problems. I lived in this camp in my first years as a pastor. Mercifully, God answered prayer and changed my ministry direction and the churches I pastored as well.

Besides this critical issue, many pastors lack the basic leadership skills of delegation and mentoring, as well as good people skills, to bring about healthy change in the systems of their churches. If you have never been mentored by a better leader than yourself or have not taken leadership classes from those who know how to do it, pursue this now. You will have to address your own leadership ability before you can master systems.

4 **You cannot create healthy church systems for your church without addressing spiritual health.** This one builds on the last. If the church itself is unhealthy spiritually, no refashioning of its systems will make an iota of difference. I know spectacularly growing churches that are one spiritual crisis away from damaging their attenders deeply. Addressing spiritual transformation is an essential ingredient for all systems. In reality, it is the foundation of all system building.

Spiritual transformation is about the church pursuing deeper intimacy with God, about believers being changed from the inside out so that they conform more and more to the likeness of Jesus (Romans 8:29). It is this continual pursuit that makes the church healthy and, in turn, its systems. When a church makes spiritual transformation foundational, then it does not take perfect systems to make the church grow. For more information on transforming lives and churches, go to www.ChurchEquippers.com.

5. Overview of the 18 Essential Systems

The purpose of this overview is to expose you to the eighteen systems that make up the biblical operation of your church. Each section starts with the Necessary Outcome stating exactly what you can expect that system to do in a healthy church. That statement also provides you with a standard by which you can evaluate the effectiveness of each system. Either it is true or it is not true of your system. If it is not, find out why and make adjustments to that system.

All church systems relate back to the vision of the church. This is the overriding issue. Either the system is helping the church accomplish its purpose (the reason why God brought it into existence) or it is not. The moment you become aware of any system that is not interconnected with the other systems to achieve the church's purpose, it must be addressed.

A general explanation of the system is included, along with critical questions that the system is answering for your church. There will be a brief breakdown of each system's major components, as well as indication of the other systems it feeds or works with symbiotically.

While I present the major components of each system, understand that a system is more than the sum of its parts. Equally important to the health of the system are the interconnections between the parts—how do they work together to make the system work effectively. Much of the interconnections are based on information exchanges that allow you to know what decisions to make or what actions to take to bring the various components together.

For example, where do evangelizing systems break down in churches? This system has seven major components. Of these, the accountability component is the critical one, because although almost every Christian confirms that he or she should obey the Great Commission, they tend to drift away from actually evangelizing because no one helps them to keep it important and central in their lives, which is what accountability is all about. The coordinator, working with the pastor and church leaders, determines where and how accountability will happen in the congregation, perhaps in the small group life, perhaps in the main weekly gathering. Without the interconnection between accountability and the other components—training, prayer and the macro-evangelism strategy—become ineffective. In spite of this vital interconnection, many churches ignore this component's function in the system. The result is evident by the lack of consistent conversion growth in those churches.

Learning interconnection between components is like learning to cook. You may know what the ingredients are for the dish you want to make. But you also have to learn how and when to combine those ingredients and how long to bake, fry or boil them to produce the food you want. Sometimes you learn this by reading a cookbook. But most people learn to cook by watching a good cook and listening to him or her. You will learn interconnections the same way; primarily by either going to observe a healthy working system in another church or by being coached by someone who knows how systems work.

Each system includes evaluation questions. The goal of the evaluation is to guide you so that you can focus your energy on learning how to build or rebuild necessary systems that will help your church increase its capacity to make and retain new disciples. This is a quantitative measuring tool, which means that you will need to measure different aspects of your systems that help indicate how healthy it is. Most measurements will be weighted from 1 to 5, although there are some 0 choices. In addition, several categories offer extra points for certain characteristics. It is crucial that you do not guess at the various levels you are asked to measure within the evaluation.

It will help you in preparation for using the evaluation questions if you rate the eighteen systems on a scale of 1-5 (1 being unhealthy and 5 being highly productive) according to your personal viewpoint about how well each system is functioning in your church. After you finish each set of evaluation questions, fill in your church's actual score and compare your answer to what you discovered.

Vision   1 2 3 4 5   Actual Score _____

Leadership   1 2 3 4 5   Actual Score _____

Decision Making   1 2 3 4 5   Actual Score _____

Evangelizing   1 2 3 4 5   Actual Score _____

Discipling   1 2 3 4 5   Actual Score _____

Gathering   1 2 3 4 5   Actual Score _____

Connection   1 2 3 4 5   Actual Score _____

Leadership Training   1 2 3 4 5   Actual Score _____

Financial   1 2 3 4 5   Actual Score _____

Facilities   1 2 3 4 5   Actual Score _____

Shepherding   1 2 3 4 5   Actual Score _____

Spiritual Life   1 2 3 4 5   Actual Score _____

Teaching   1 2 3 4 5   Actual Score _____

Communication   1 2 3 4 5   Actual Score _____

Community Relations   1 2 3 4 5   Actual Score _____

Small Groups   1 2 3 4 5   Actual Score _____

Ministries   1 2 3 4 5   Actual Score _____

Missions   1 2 3 4 5   Actual Score _____

I encourage you to use this evaluation to your advantage by not fudging the numbers in the survey. It will not serve you or your church to indicate your systems are healthier than they really are. Take the time to count well. Understand that any system that scores below 3.0 is stressed or even counterproductive for the church. As you examine these particular systems, know that a lot of aspects of the system may be functioning fine, but missing significant components.

More explanation of systems evaluation can be found in Appendix 1.

You can go to www.churchequippers.com/systems for further information and training on healthy church systems.

SYSTEM 1: VISION

Necessary Outcome: *We are united and moving forward towards accomplishing a common godly purpose.*

Introduction

When I was learning how to lead a church, vision stood for what kind of church model you wanted to imitate and interpreting the area demographics where your church was located. It represented the best ideas about how to do church effectively in one's community and came with a three to five year plan. For some pastors, vision is a number as in, "We are going to reach 100 new people this year." Or they would talk in terms of their church's preferred future.

What vision is to Jesus is quite different. He was twisted with compassion when he saw the crowds because they were as confused and helpless as sheep without a shepherd (Matthew 9:36). Jesus' response is the essence of vision. Vision is what moves you to compassion and proclamation of the gospel as a result of seeing the great needs of the people in the community where God has sent you.

Like Paul's dream at Troas of the Macedonian man begging for help, vision is a revelation from God and not your best ideas or your personal preferences. Vision is the reason God has you in the community you are called to serve as a church. It comes to a leader or a team through prayer and observations about the community, as well as the church's resources and passion.

Vision is the DNA of the church God has called you to lead. If you think of the church as a cell, the vision is the nucleus of that cell, defining its purpose, strategies and functions. A church without a vision is just a collection of people, all doing what is right in their own eyes but not necessarily accomplishing much together. All the other church systems connect and draw their purpose from this vision.

Why many churches fail to attain their potential and remain small (85% of all churches are under 200 people, 60% are under 100) is because the leaders do not embrace the demandingness of the vision God is giving them. A vision is like the marching orders of the church. While this may seem obvious, the majority of churches drift towards lowering the bar of partnership so that people can be part of the church without owning its vision. Such churches end up with attenders who do just that—attend without involvement in the mission of the church. A number of these people (perhaps most) will suck up resources without giving back as if the church exists merely to serve them.

A healthy church understands that its mission is tied to its vision and only people who want to join it in pursuing the vision will be at home. Others who already are believers will be encouraged to join with them and, if they are not interested in the

36

vision, asked to find another church to attend. New believers will be discipled to prepare them to be co-workers in the church's vision. One church I know started in the tough neighborhood of their city, reaching children from streets where drugs and violence were not uncommon. They are bringing hope to homeless people. Not for the faint hearted. In another city, one of my friends leads a church which is consistently reaching 25-32 years olds through unique means and in unique places. You have to want to do this in order to be part of it.

The vision needs to be taught to the launch team from the beginning of a new church. Renewed vision needs to be owned by the leadership of an established church as soon as it is received from God and understood. It defines the culture of the congregation and guides its decision about which ministries and missions it will pursue.

Critical Questions This System Answers:

- What is it that this church is supposed to do for the Kingdom at this time in this place?
- Why is this church supposed to do it?
- How is this church planning to get this done?
- What markers will tell this church that it is succeeding in its vision?

Major Components:

Theology: A clarifying statement of your Ecclesiology and Christology is foundational to any vision system. Your theology defines what kind of church you will raise and/or lead.

Discovery Process: Through which the Spirit gives you insight into the community, your co-workers and your apostolic passion. From these three discoveries you will come to know the vision God has for you to pursue.

Vision Statement: A brief, but thorough, statement that explains why this church is here in this community and to whom God has sent it to sow the gospel. This statement becomes the standard that defines the church's mission.

Non-Negotiables: The beliefs, actions and attitudes that define the church you are forming and/or leading. These must be embraced by all who belong if the church is going to be the church you are called to lead.

Vision Strategy: The pathway by which the church will accomplish its vision. This can be written or unwritten, but it must be transferable to others who join with you.

Strategy Evaluation: Dates and means by which the vision strategy is timely reviewed and measured to know that the church is on course or whether the leaders need to change course.

Vision Celebrations: Scheduled weekly, monthly and yearly times when the congregation praises God for His work through and among them.

Vision Communication: Means by which the congregation is taught or reminded of the vision God has given them for the community.

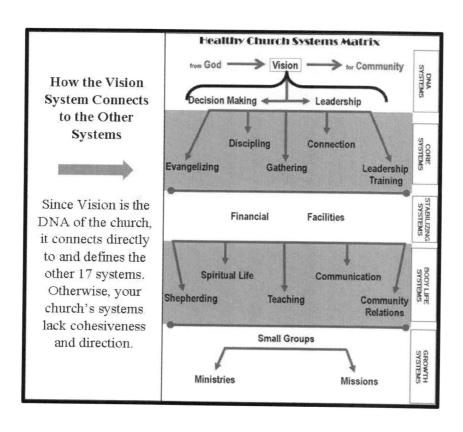

VISION SYSTEM SURVEY QUESTIONS

Written Vision

1 _____ The church has no clarifying vision statement that defines the reason God has us in this community.

2 _____ A survey of the congregation indicates that less than 10% can recite the vision statement.

3 _____ A survey of the congregation indicates at least 25% know the vision of the church.

4 _____ A survey of the congregation indicates more than 50 % know the vision of the church.

5 _____ A survey of the congregation indicates more than 75% know the vision of the church.

Written Strategy

1 _____ The church has no written strategy for implementing our vision.

2 _____ The church has a written strategy for implementing this vision, but less than 25% of our ministries are aligned with our vision.

3 _____ The church has a written strategy for implementing this vision, but less than 50% of our ministries are aligned with our vision.

4 _____ The church has a written strategy for implementing this vision and 50-75% of our ministries align with our vision.

5 _____ The church has a written strategy for implementing this vision and more than 75% of our ministries align with our vision.

Ministry Evaluation

1 _____ The church does not practice a yearly ministry evaluation process to make sure that our ministries are aligned with the vision.

3 _____ The church practices a ministry evaluation process every other year to make sure that our ministries are aligned with the vision.

5 _____ The church practices a yearly ministry evaluation process to make sure that our ministries are aligned with the vision.

Evaluation Markers

1 _____ The church has no way to evaluate our ministries against strategy.

2 _____ The church is hitting less than 25% of our evaluation markers.

3 _____ The church is hitting at least 25-50% of our yearly evaluation markers.

4 _____ The church is hitting at least 50-75% of our yearly evaluation markers.

5 _____ The church is hitting at least 75-90% of our yearly evaluation markers.

Celebration

1 _____   The church does not have any focused celebration over achieving our vision strategy.

2 _____   The church has at least one planned celebration time a year over achieving our vision strategy.

3 _____   The church has three to five celebration times a year over achieving some aspect of our vision strategy.

4 _____   The church has a monthly celebration over achieving some aspect of our vision strategy.

5 _____   The church has a weekly celebration over achieving some aspect of our vision strategy.

Growth

1 _____   The church has experienced less than 5% growth for each of the last three years.

2 _____   The church has experienced 5% growth for one year out of the last three years.

3 _____   The church has experienced 5% growth for each of the last three years.

4 _____   The church has experienced 10% growth for one year out of the last three years.

5 _____   The church has experienced 10%+ growth for each of the last three years.

Total _____ divided by 6 = _____

SYSTEM 2: LEADERSHIP

Necessary Outcome: *A growing group of spirit-filled, wise people are guiding all aspects of our mission.*

Introduction

The Leadership System is at the heart of making sure the church is capable to do its ministry. I know of a church that has a congregation of over 500 attenders, but only one vocational pastor on staff. Looking in from the outside, you might wonder how one person can possibly handle the demands of so many. But if you look closer, you will discover that this pastor has a masterful Leadership System. Much of the ministry work is being done by leaders he has trained and empowered. What he has is a "Jethro" system of leadership, based on the plan Moses' father-in-law explained to him in Exodus 18.

Probably the biggest aspect of any church being able to increase capacity is their plan for an expandable leadership "skeleton." The Jethro model is *one* way of visualizing this skeleton. In it you have small ministry leaders, who are leaders of people (i.e. leaders of 10), large ministry and development leaders, who function as leaders of leaders (i.e. leaders of 50) and those who operate as either lay or vocational staff, leading the church (i.e. leaders of 100). Leaders of 1000 only come into play when the church begins to make the transition from a church of 500 to a church of 1000+. These leaders function as visionaries and provide focal point leadership to other top leaders.

Why do you need a leadership skeleton? First, you need one because as you go forward, you must delegate responsibility to emerging leaders of 50 or you will be swamped with too many direct reports. Trying to maintain a flat organization with everyone coming to you as the leader will eventually eat up all your time and kill you or the church's momentum towards growth.

Second, having a skeleton means that you are planning to exercise quality control over important ministries. This also contributes to increasing capacity. Quality control is different from micro-managing. Micro-managing means an overseer is really running the ministry instead of its leader. Quality control is making sure a ministry stays on course according to its intended purpose and in harmony with the church's vision. A leadership skeleton assures that no ministry leader of 10 or leader of 50 lacks someone who knows what they are to do and is in close view of their ministry work for the church.

Third, this approach to leadership provides a pathway to grow in ministry. Faithfulness and fruitfulness at the leader of 10 level will make that person available to advance in responsibility if he or she desires that opportunity. This leadership skeleton also provides a natural pathway towards mentoring every level of leaders. The expectation is that the leader at the next level will be the mentor for the leaders under his or her responsibility.

Your church needs all levels of leaders. The Jethro Leadership System is based on the rule of thumb that you will need one leader for every ten attenders and one leader over every five leaders. These are estimates but the truth is, the more leaders you have, the better you can keep the church's small groups, ministries and missions (Growth Systems) from drifting away from the vision. Keep in mind that one of the functions of leadership is to create more leaders so that the work of the church can expand. A second function of leadership is to resolve challenges facing the church in following its vision. These two factors make up the core of the Leadership System and can be addressed through a good leadership skeleton.

If you are leading an existing church, you need to determine the proportion of leaders you currently have. This gives you a clear picture of what your goals for this system will be. If you are starting a new church, you must think in terms of how many leaders you will need as you launch and grow the church.

Critical Questions This System Answers:

- Do we have the right people at the top leadership level?
- Do we have a plan to develop leaders so that they grow in leadership?
- Are we staffed in leadership for growth—by which is meant that we have more qualified leaders in all levels than we need at the size of the congregation we are at the moment?

Major Components:

Leaders' Responsibilities: The basic expectations of what all leaders are to do in the church and what sacrifices will be asked of them as they serve the Kingdom are clarified.

Agenda Harmony: The standard of agreement over the church's vision is set out for all leaders.

Job Descriptions: These are the written general job descriptions for all leaders of 10, 50, 100 and 1000, including what authority they have and how their position fits into the overall structure.

Mentoring Plan: A process is developed in which all leaders are engaged in developing co-workers as well as their own replacements.

Advanced Training: A pathway is determined for those who lead to constantly hone their skills and deepen their knowledge of God and His Kingdom.

Yearly Expectations: The who, how and when yearly ministry expectations are developed for all leaders.

Leadership Failure Plan: A clear plan how the leaders will deal with someone who fails in leadership or falls into sin.

Staff Philosophy: The philosophy of hiring staff for the church is clarified.

Top Leadership Requirements: Means by which your top leadership team members are identified and recruited.

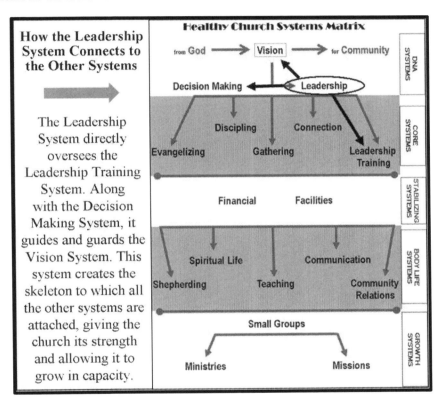

How the Leadership System Connects to the Other Systems

The Leadership System directly oversees the Leadership Training System. Along with the Decision Making System, it guides and guards the Vision System. This system creates the skeleton to which all the other systems are attached, giving the church its strength and allowing it to grow in capacity.

LEADERSHIP SYSTEM SURVEY QUESTIONS

Leaders

1 _____   The leadership of our church consists of the pastor and other leaders totaling less than 5% of the attenders who pretty much have to run every ministry.

2 _____   Our trained leadership to attender ratio is 1 to 20 or 5%.

3 _____   Our trained leadership to attender ratio is 1 to 10 or 10%.

4 _____   In addition to having a 10% trained leadership to attender ratio, The church has a leader of leaders to leaders ratio of 1 to 10 or 10%.

5 _____   In addition to having a trained leadership to attender ratio better than 10%, The church has a minimum leader of leaders to leaders ratio of 1 to 5 or 20%+.

Alignment

1 _____   The church has at least two top leaders who are not in agreement with the vision and direction of the church.

2 _____   The church has at least one top leader who is not in agreement with the vision and direction of the church.

3 _____   All our top leaders agree about a common vision for our church, but the church has more than two people leading at the next level who are not in agreement with the vision and direction of the church.

4 _____   All our top leaders agree about a common vision for our church, but the church has a person leading at the next level who is not in agreement with the vision and direction of the church.

5 _____   All leaders at every level are in agreement about a common vision for our church.

Responsibilities

1 _____   The church has no written leadership job descriptions for any leader outside the pastor and our governing board.

3 _____   The church has written leadership job descriptions for all leaders of 10 and 50 positions.

5 _____   The church has written leadership job descriptions for all leaders of 10, 50, and 100 positions.

Training

1 _____   The church has no process for developing new leaders.

2 _____   The church offers some classes in leadership.

3 _____   At least ten classroom sessions a year are offered to those interested in leadership.

4 _____   Besides classes, the church has initiated a mentoring process by which leaders are training someone to learn to lead on the job.

5 _____   Besides classes and mentoring, the church offers 1-2 courses in advanced leadership and biblical/theological training for leaders a year.

Ministry Growth

1 _____   The church has either had to stop ministries in the last 24 months or not start crucial ministries as defined by our vision strategy for lack of qualified leaders.

2 _____   The church has been able to launch 1-2 new ministries this year using people who are already involved in another ministry or were part of a ministry that ended.

3 _____   The church has been able to launch 3-5 new ministries or cover the loss of critical leaders due to having extra leaders this year.

4 _____   The church has been able to launch more than 6 new ministries to cover the loss of critical leaders due to having extra leaders this year.

5 _____   The church has been able to launch more than 6 new ministries this year plus supply numerous leaders for our daughter church.

Service

1 _____   Each leader in our church gives 1-3 hours of service beyond attending the weekly gathering.

3 _____   Each leader of 10 in our church gives 1-3 hours of service and each leader of 50 gives 3-5 hours of service beyond attending the weekly gathering.

5 _____   Each leader of 50 gives 5-10 hours of service and each leader of 100 gives 10+ hours of service beyond attending the weekly gathering.

Bonus

+2 _____ All of the leaders have a written copy of the church's expectations and goals for the next year.

Total _____ divided by 6 = _____

SYSTEM 3: DECISION MAKING

Necessary Outcome: *The congregation feels that all decisions made are appropriate, clear and are implemented with proper authority.*

Introduction

I was with a leader who coaches leaders of church planting movements all around the globe. He wanted to know more about church systems and structure. As we were looking at the Healthy Church Systems Matrix, he surprised me with the outburst, "There is a system for decision making!" He explained the reason for his excitement was that he was dealing with a leadership team in Belarus who were fighting over this very issue. How were decisions supposed to be made? And, more importantly, who got the final say? This leader was delighted to see that there was a way to teach them what they needed to know.

You need to have a strong Decision Making System to make sure that your congregation feels that all decisions are appropriate, clear and implemented with proper authority. In other words, you want your attenders to trust you and your leaders and you want to make sure that you have the freedom to make the right decisions. This is why decision making is one of the DNA Systems grouped with vision and leadership. Your church's vision needs both leaders who are all going in the same direction and a way to protect the vision from people thinking they can vote it out!

Agreement on vision and direction among leaders, however, does not necessarily translate into rubber-stamped decisions. Nor does it mean that all decisions will be good and right. Agenda harmony does mean that the path has been cleared to listen and learn from each other so that collaborative decisions can be made.

Protecting the vision of your church is the crucial role of the Decision Making System. If you develop it right, it prevents people outside the leadership of the church from realigning its vision away from the direction God has revealed. This is not to say that no one but the leaders have a part in making decisions. Instead, the

Decision Making System defines the different levels in which staff, leaders, and the congregation participate in the process of deciding the various issues every church faces.

Answering the question of who should be in on decisions starts with a firm understanding of what decisions you are addressing. There are four kinds of decisions that have to be made all the time in churches. They are: 1) major ministry decisions; 2) daily ministry decisions; 3) major financial decisions; and 4) daily financial decisions. Your top leadership team will be responsible for a number of the major decisions, but a healthy growing church assigns many of the daily decisions to others who are leading the various ministries. Also, for certain decisions, the top leadership will need to ask the whole church to give input. How these decisions are allotted to whom depends on how you develop your system.

The second important function of the Decision Making System is it assures that the leaders of the church have proper accountability. Since there is no one right way to be accountable, this system guides the leadership in determining to whom and to what degree they are to be held accountable, whether internally or externally. It gives a positive answer the question, "Who do you want to look over your shoulder?" Accountability prevents the pastor, staff and top leadership from leading the church unwittingly, but dangerously, towards destruction.

What I have discovered is that this system is flexible and capable of change as the church grows. For example, at the start of a new church, the planter generally does not know who will emerge as the key leaders. Leadership in a new church takes time to develop. Even good leaders in another church may not lead well in this new church. For the first several years in a new church, the planter may retain decision-making responsibilities until he knows that he has the right co-leaders for this church. Otherwise, he could find himself unable to move the church plant forward in a timely and decisive fashion.

For an established church ready to move from one size level to the next, the critical issue for your Decision Making System is that the speed at which major decisions need to be made by nature increases. Otherwise the growth process could be compromised. The goal is to be able to make faster decisions wisely and with accountability.

Critical Questions This System Answers:

- Who makes the final decision in our church?
- What decisions should the congregation make?
- To whom are we accountable?

Major Components:

Major Decision Approval: What constitutes a major decision and who has the final say over them is determined.

Other Decisions Approval: Which decisions are to be made by ministry leaders and which ones will be made by the congregation is decided.

Permission Giving: Determining how much appropriate and necessary authority will be delegated down to leaders, speeding up the decision-making process in the church.

Leadership Meeting Focus: Guidelines on how you will utilize your time together in sorting out the top leadership decisions is created for the top leadership team.

Accountability: To whom and under how much accountability will be the pastor and the top leadership is determined.

Record Keeping: Description about how the top leadership team will record and communicate decisions.

Guiding Documents: The purpose of these documents is to explain the process of decision making and to report the previous decisions that currently guide the life of the congregation so that new people will know how your church operates. These include policy manuals, by-laws and the church's constitution.

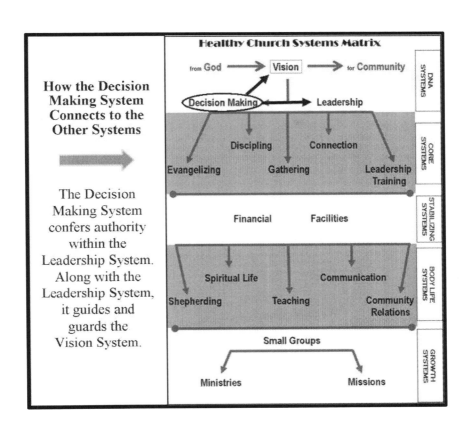

How the Decision Making System Connects to the Other Systems

The Decision Making System confers authority within the Leadership System. Along with the Leadership System, it guides and guards the Vision System.

DECISION MAKING SYSTEM SURVEY QUESTIONS

Timing

1 _____   The majority of the financial and ministry decisions take more than one month to be made.

3 _____   The majority of the financial and ministry decisions take three to four weeks to be made.

5 _____   All decisions are made within the week unless there is a crisis.

Decision Participants

1 _____   All ministry financial decisions (major and daily) are handled by the pastor.

3 _____   All ministry financial decisions (major and daily) are handled through the leadership team.

5 _____ Daily ministry and financial decisions are made by a ministry leader of 50, who are accountable to the top leadership team.

Congregational Knowledge of Process

0 _____ Only the top leaders know the church's decision making policy.

1 _____ It is required that all leaders know the decision making policy.

3 _____ Understanding the decision making policy is part of the membership training, therefore at least 25% of our attenders having knowledge of the process.

5 _____ Understanding the decision making policy is part of the membership training, therefore more than 50% of our attenders having knowledge of the process.

Accountability

1 _____ The church leadership has no outside authority to consult for accountability.

3 _____ The church leadership has identified and is accountable in some way to an outside authority.

5 _____ The church leadership has a written policy about its accountability to an outside authority.

Policies

1 _____ The church has no written policy manual.

3 _____ Policies are being written down as needed.

5 _____ There is a comprehensive policy manual that guides the leaders.

Bonus

+1 _____ The decision making process has freed the pastor to participate in broader ministry to other people and organizations outside the church.

Total _____ divided by 5 = _____

SYSTEM 4: EVANGELIZING

Necessary Outcome: *Disciples are regularly witnessing to others, resulting in consistent conversion growth in the church.*

Introduction

There are only two ways to grow a church aside from a baby explosion among your young couples. Churches gain new people either from transfer growth or conversion growth. While all churches like to see new people joining the congregation, growth does not necessarily indicate that your church is fulfilling its vision. It may mean that you have become a repository of 'already Christians' who like the worship, the preaching or the programs. If your church is to realize the purpose for which God has brought it into existence, you will need to develop an effective Evangelizing System. System here means more than creating an evangelistic approach. It means creating an *evangelizing culture* where all the people in your congregation live to share the gospel with those around them intentionally through their lives and words, because they are full to overflowing with gratitude for what God has done for each of them though Jesus.

Evangelizing is half of the Great Commission, the part that is the proclamation of the good news about Jesus. An Evangelizing System is not about whether or not you, the leader, personally are able to share the good news about Jesus, either through your preaching or witness. The function of this system is to help the church to become evangelistically effective.

The primary question the Evangelizing System is asking and then answering is: *"What are the faith-sharing connection points between lost people and the people who make up this congregation?"* It is estimated that less than 5% of all Christians in the USA ever lead anyone to faith in Jesus. One of the contributing factors to this unhappy statistic is that most Christ-followers have few non-believers as their friends. Non-believers who your attenders know are accorded very little relational time, as most believers prefer the society of other Christians. Changing this reality is a primary part of developing a healthy Evangelizing System.

The second question this system addresses is: *"How does this congregation work together to reach lost people with the gospel?"* A church that does not have a game plan to evangelizing the lost together is engaging in wishful thinking, because most people need the structure of a team in order to stay engaged in evangelism. A healthy church has more than one macro-evangelism strategy and encourages segments of the congregation to develop strategies for their workplace, neighborhood and city. Whatever strategy the church pursues, this system is clearly at the center of the congregation's fulfilling its vision. All strategies that the church develops should bear that in mind, so that the people for whom they have compassion are at the focus of these strategies.

Critical Questions This System Answers:

- Is our understanding of the gospel sufficient?
- Do those we baptize yearly equal 10% of our attendance?

Major Components:

Gospel: The church must have a clear and comprehensively defined understanding of the gospel to inform believers and guide their proclamation.

Training: The process in which people are properly prepared to be witnesses. This can be a formal or informal process.

Prayer: Times and means by which people pray individually and corporately for the lost.

Accountability: Accountability is making evangelizing important. This component describes the method used to make sure people are actually staying engaged in sharing the gospel.

Macro-Evangelism Strategy: Both the central and auxiliary approaches that the congregation uses to proclaim the gospel into the community and reap a harvest together.

Baptism: The church's theological position and practice concerning the relationship between salvation and the act of baptism.

Coordinator: A recruiting tool for finding the person who oversees this system.

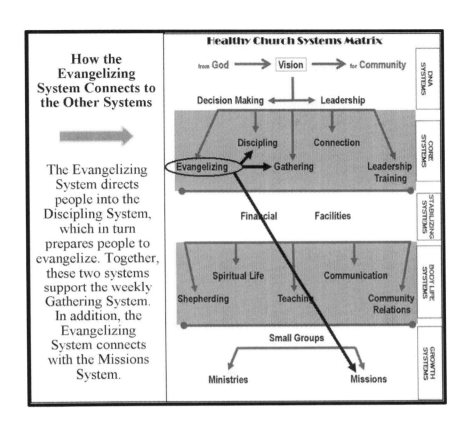

How the Evangelizing System Connects to the Other Systems

The Evangelizing System directs people into the Discipling System, which in turn prepares people to evangelize. Together, these two systems support the weekly Gathering System. In addition, the Evangelizing System connects with the Missions System.

Healthy Church Systems Matrix

from God → Vision → for Community

DNA SYSTEMS

Decision Making ↔ Leadership

Discipling   Connection

Evangelizing → Gathering   Leadership Training

CORE SYSTEMS

Financial   Facilities

STABILIZING SYSTEMS

Spiritual Life   Communication

Shepherding   Teaching   Community Relations

BODY LIFE SYSTEMS

Small Groups

Ministries   Missions

GROWTH SYSTEMS

EVANGELIZING SYSTEM SURVEY QUESTIONS

Training Participation

1 ___ Except for a few individuals, no one has been trained in evangelism nor is a training class offered.

2 ___ A training class in evangelism is offered at least once a year, with 10% of the congregation having been through the training.

3 ___ 25% of the congregation has been through the church's training process on evangelism.

4 ___ 50% of the congregation has been through the church's training process on evangelism.

5 ___ More than 75% of the congregation has been through the church's training process on evangelism.

Conversion Growth

1 _____   Aside from baptizing children of members, yearly conversion growth is less than 1 person baptized per 50 members per year.

2 _____   Yearly conversion growth is 1 person baptized per 50 members.

3 _____   Yearly conversion growth is 1 person baptized per 30 members.

4 _____   Yearly conversion growth is 1 person baptized per 20 members.

5 _____   Yearly conversion growth is more than 1 person baptized per 10 members.

Retention (those who do not move from the community)

1 _____   The church has retained less than 25% of new believers over the last five years.

2 _____   The church has retained between 25-49% of new believers over the last five years.

3 _____   The church has retained between 50-74% of new believers over the last five years.

4 _____   The church has retained between 75-98% of new believers over the last five years.

5 _____   The church has retained more than 90% of new believers over the last five years.

Discipleship

1 _____   The church has no process for moving new believers from baptism to discipleship.

2 _____   Up to 25% of the new believers have entered our discipleship process.

3 _____   Up to 50% of the new believers have entered our discipleship process.

4 _____   Up to 75% of the new believers have entered our discipleship process.

5 _____   Up to 90% or more of the new believers have entered our discipleship process.

1 _____   Either the pastor or his wife coordinates this system or no one is assigned to oversee it.

2 _____   An untrained volunteer oversees this system.

3 _____   A trained leader over volunteers oversees this system.

4 _____   A dedicated leader leads other leaders and a team in overseeing this system.

5 _____   A dedicated leader mentoring his or her replacement and a team oversees this system.

Total _____ divided by 5 = _____

SYSTEM 5: DISCIPLING

Necessary Outcome: *Disciples are pursuing God, conforming to the likeness of Jesus and growing into co-workers in the Kingdom.*

Introduction

A premier pastor of a former generation was mentoring a group of younger leaders of which I was part. During one of his discussions he mentioned that in the years since he retired from ministry he had visited over 250 churches all around the country and never had seen a comprehensive Discipling System in any of them. He saw this as one of the great weaknesses of the church of today.

In truth, churches are discipling people, but not in a way that produces great results. Instead of a carefully thought through approach that recognizes what it means to teach new believers to obey everything Jesus taught us, both through the Word and through living it out before them, many churches' discipling process has a catch-as-catch-can feel to it. With no clear guidelines, each new believer has to figure out for him or herself what they need to know. For many, they just look at the lives of the other church attenders and within six months, they have learned all they think they need to know. I wish this were an exaggeration.

This is a major reason why developing your Discipling System is so critical. Many people who are currently populating your church have not been well discipled. This is not just true of young believers. People in major leadership roles often have serious deficiencies in their learning to obey everything Jesus taught. When you realize that the goal of discipling is to lead believers towards ongoing transformation into the image of Jesus, then you will begin to take the development of your discipling approach very seriously. It should never be left to chance nor should you believe that the disciple will discover what he or she needs to know without your guidance.

Discipling is the second half of the Great Commission. Clearly, merely guiding someone to believe and be baptized is not the end of the process of making disciples. Like evangelizing, your ultimate goal is to create a discipling culture, where everyone is not only seeking to grow in their knowledge of God and His grace, but are putting it out there for all younger believers as well. Although you may develop teaching components for certain parts of your process, people learn to follow Jesus from other followers (and not just the pastor!).

Critical to long-term success of any discipling process is awareness that most—not all—discipleship material starts with four faulty assumptions. These assumptions, if not realized and addressed, will produce weaker disciples who will someday and in some way question their faith. These four assumptions are: 1) New believers understand the process of sanctification, which is the work of the Spirit in their lives, saving them from the power of sin. This is so often assumed that some materials never even mention it. 2) New believers automatically trust God with their lives. Surprisingly, many do not trust God and do not even know why. 3) New believers believe the Bible has complete authority to guide them. Most new believers have precious little biblical knowledge and have been exposed to cultural debates denigrating what the Bible says on numerous subjects. Yet much discipleship material plunges new believers right into looking up biblical passages, expecting them to accept scriptural truth. 4) New believers understand and embrace a biblical worldview—God is creator of all and reigns over His creation, evil in the world is the result of rebellion, humankind and the world itself has been affected by this fall, etc.—after confessing faith. This is wishful thinking. Seek materials that address these issues if you want to develop strong disciples.

And don't just think in terms of adults. I was personally challenged a number of years ago by a teacher who reminded his class that we often reserve discipling for adult believers. He pointed out that churches had the opportunity to invest years of discipling into children and teens who grow up within the congregation. But often churches fumbled on this, having no comprehensive plan beyond teaching children Bible stories or the teens a lot of the 'how to' issues that come up for them. I pass on his challenge to think through a clear discipling pathway for your non-adults or you will see the tragedy that happens in too many churches, kids leaving the faith because it is not *their* faith. And while they may return years later, they still will lack discipling in their lives.

The challenge is to develop new believers from the acorn to the oak. I find that this is the hardest system for most leaders to put together because very few of them have ever been through a discipling process themselves. So they have no template to look back on to guide them in putting this system together. I have had this statement confirmed over and over by pastors with whom I work. However, once pastors develop a discipling process, they find it is one of the easiest systems to implement.

Critical Questions This System Answers:

- What are the pieces of our discipleship process?
- Where in our church life do we do the pieces in our discipleship process?
- How do we do the pieces of our discipleship process?
- How often do we offer each piece of our discipleship process?
- Who is responsible for each piece of our discipleship process?

Major Components:

Spiritual Transformation: The heart of discipling is people being progressively transformed by the gospel. This component determines how the church will make this central to the process.

End Product: A thoroughly scriptural description of what a mature disciple should look like.

Delivery System: Where, how and by what means the church will offer the various parts of the discipling process.

Process Calendaring: What is not on the calendar does not exist. The issue for a church is to find a place for all discipling units in a repeatable cycle.

Communication: How the church will communicate the expectation for all believers to complete this process and lead others in this process.

Discipler Training: A training plan is developed for preparing people as disciplers for your church.

Teen Discipling: Process by which teens are taught to be intimate with God and prepared to serve in the kingdom.

Children Discipling: Process by which children are taught to be intimate with God and prepared to serve in the kingdom.

Coordinator: A recruiting tool for finding the person who oversees this system.

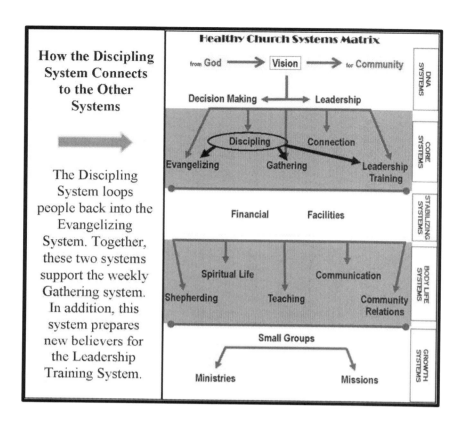

How the Discipling System Connects to the Other Systems

The Discipling System loops people back into the Evangelizing System. Together, these two systems support the weekly Gathering system. In addition, this system prepares new believers for the Leadership Training System.

Healthy Church Systems Matrix

DISCIPLING SYSTEM SURVEY QUESTIONS

Process

1 _____   The church has no defined process of discipling new believers.

2 _____   The church has a 3-6 month discipling process developed for new believers.

3 _____   The church has a 9-15 month discipling process developed for new believers.

4 _____   The church has a 18-24 month discipling process developed for new believers.

5 _____   The church has implemented a discipling process for teens and children.

Content

1 ____   There are no designated courses that new disciples are expected to take.

2 ____   Disciples are offered Christian life courses and Bible classes.

3 ____   Disciples are expected to take entry level biblical and theological knowledge courses.

4 ____   Disciples are expected to take entry level spiritual transformation foundations training as well as the biblical and theological knowledge courses.

5 ____   Entry level and advanced spiritual transformation and biblical knowledge/world view training is offered.

New Believer Participation

1 ____   Over the last five years, less than 25% of new believers received some kind of discipling.

2 ____   Over the last five years, 25-49% of new believers have entered into this process.

3 ____   Over the last five years, 50-74% of new believers have entered into this process.

4 ____   Over the last five years, 75-89% of new believers have entered into this process.

5 ____   Over the last five years, more than 90% of new believers have entered into this process.

Mature Believer Participation

1 ____   The pastor and his wife engage in discipling new believers.

2 ____   The pastor and a few leaders of the church engage in discipling new believers.

3 ____   10% of the members have been trained and are engaged in discipling new believers.

4 ____   30% of the members have been trained and are engaged in discipling new believers.

| 5 ___ | 50% of the members have been trained and are engaged in discipling new believers. |

Leader

1 ___	Either the pastor or his wife coordinates this system or no one is assigned to oversee it.
2 ___	An untrained volunteer oversees this system.
3 ___	A trained leader over volunteers oversees this system.
4 ___	A dedicated leader leads other leaders and a team in overseeing this system.
5 ___	A dedicated leader mentoring his or her replacement and a team oversees this system.

Total _____ divided by 5 = _____

SYSTEM 6: GATHERING

Necessary Outcome: *Disciples come together with an expectation that they are in God's presence and are growing in love, community and passion.*

Introduction

By biblical definition, churches are the people of the Lord gathered, not the building in which they gather. When believers come together in community, they are the church, whether in a small group or in a large congregation. These gatherings are both natural and desirable, as they are the times when the people can both worship God together and encourage each other.

Many churches give a lot of time in developing their weekly gathering. That does not mean their gatherings are effective. As a person who oversees churches, I have sat through many gatherings in various cultures. Some gatherings felt incredibly long and others seemed to fly by. The amount of time was not the issue. The ones that flew by had the people most engaged both in the worship and the Word portions of the gathering. The various parts of the gathering both raised the attenders' awareness of God's presence and led them further in confident hope of being transformed.

It's no surprise that what you do with the gathering time will impact your church's ability to increase capacity. Since the weekly all-church gathering is the focal point for the church, the spiritual temperature and the care and thought that goes into these times affect the growth of the congregation. But the growing in capacity issues are interconnected with several other systems—Spiritual Life, Facilities, Evangelizing and Ministries (in this case, specifically the quality of your children's ministry). So increased capacity is not just about more space. It touches the broader health of the church, especially in its faith life.

When approaching this system, the challenge is to put aside one's conditioned thinking. All leaders have some idea how a gathering should be conducted from their own experience. But to build an effective system, one must start with evaluating the congregation. Who are attending and why? What motivates their worship of God? How do they learn from the Word? How will this time move them forward in their faith journey? From the church itself a powerful gathering time can be developed.

Critical Questions This System Answers:

- What do we expect our gathering times to accomplish?
- What do we want to happen during our gatherings that will move people towards God in passion and towards each other in community?

Major Components:

Congregational Evaluation: A clear statement of who makes up the congregation and what they need to help them worship God together.

Theology of Worship: A definition of the theology of worship that shapes how the church will approach God in worship.

Worship Concept: Clarifying explanation about what constitutes worship, guiding the church in its ability to distinguish the qualities it seeks in a worship leader.

Core Practices: A list of core practices around which worship time revolves.

Planning: How and when the worship team will plan the church's gathering time.

Preaching/Teaching: The function of preaching/teaching in the church's gatherings is determined.

Next Steps Guidance: A guideline in how the leaders will use the gathering time to guide people in the next steps of their faith journey.

Evaluation Form: Knowing what is working or not working at a gathering can be difficult to discern as a participant. This component guides in developing an evaluation form so that the team receives feedback regularly.

Coordinator: A recruiting tool for finding the person who oversees this system and for those who will be part of the worship team.

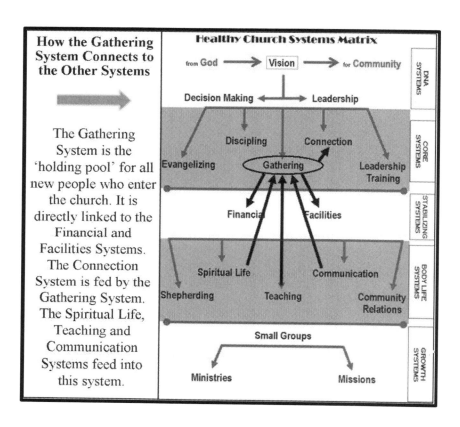

GATHERING SYSTEM SURVEY QUESTIONS

Participation of Those Who Are Part of the Congregation

1 ____   Less than 50% attend the church's gatherings at least 3 out of 4 times a month.

2 ____   50% attend the church's gathering at least 3 out of 4 times a month.

3 ____   60% attend the church's gathering at least 3 out of 4 times a month.

4 _____   70% attend the church's gathering at least 3 out of 4 times a month.

5 _____   80% attend the church's gathering at least 3 out of 4 times a month.

Worship

1 _____   The church uses video worship music or has a volunteer musician to lead the worship.

2 _____   The church has a lone trained worship leader who leads the worship.

3 _____   The church has a consistent team working with a trained worship leader to lead the worship.

4 _____   The church has 2 worship teams to lead the worship.

5 _____   The church has 3 or more worship teams to lead the worship.

Visitors

1 _____   The church averages less than 1 visitor per 100 attenders a month.

2 _____   The church averages 5-10 visitors per 100 attenders a month.

3 _____   The church averages 3-5 visitors per 100 attenders a week.

4 _____   The church averages 6-10 visitors per 100 attenders a week.

5 _____   The church averages more than 11 visitors per 100 attenders a week.

Invitation

1 _____   Attenders rarely invite people to visit our gathering.

2 _____   25% of our visitors are invited by members.

3 _____   50% of our visitors are invited by members.

4 _____   60% of our visitors are invited by members.

5 _____   75% of our visitors are invited by members.

Flow to Growth Systems

1 _____   Less than 10% of the gathering attenders also participate in one or more of our growth systems (small group, ministries, missions).

2 ___	Up to 25% of the gathering attenders also participate in one or more of our growth systems (small group, ministries, missions).
3 ___	Up to 50% of the gathering attenders also participate in one or more of our growth systems (small group, ministries, missions).
4 ___	Up to 70% of the gathering attenders also participate in one or more of our growth systems (small group, ministries, missions).
5 ___	Up to 80% of the gathering attenders also participate in one or more of our growth systems (small group, ministries, missions).

Leader

1 ___	The pastor or his wife plans the gathering
3 ___	The pastor and the worship leader plan the gathering.
5 ___	A team plans the gathering in coordination with the pastor.

Total _____ divided by 6 = _____

SYSTEM 7: CONNECTION

Necessary Outcome: *New people regularly unite in the community life of the congregation.*

Introduction

If you want to retain those who come into your gatherings, this is a critical system for you. Connection means enfolding into the congregation the people God sends to you. In preparing to connect with new people, two questions must be answered to develop a healthy Connection System. People who visit are asking these unspoken questions: *"Am I wanted?"* and *"Am I needed?"* If you intentionally answer these questions adequately within a reasonable period, you will retain more of your visitors.

Visitors may say they came to your gathering for a variety of reasons, but the real reason they are there is that the Holy Spirit drew them to your gathering that morning. You have the opportunity to connect them to the congregation so that hopefully they will stay to hear and receive the gospel over time, becoming mature disciples and co-workers with you in the Kingdom. Before they come, you need to prepare all connection team members, as well as your entire congregation, to be ready to answer the question, "*Am I wanted?*"

But let's keep this simple. The goal of a good Connection System is to lead visitors from their first visit to their becoming part of one of your Growth Systems as quickly as feasible. This means that if your connection team can move new people into a small group, ministry or mission within the first months of their arrival, they will find deepening relationships (*Am I wanted?*) and get a chance to serve others in some capacity (*Am I needed?*). Making this the ultimate goal means that you have to pay attention to your Growth Systems if you want to increase your church's capacity for retaining visitors. Moreover, to increase the number of small groups, ministries and missions, you have to develop more leaders of 10/50 to fuel this increase. These systems are interlocked, so the failure in one will trigger loss in the others. Keep that in mind when you evaluate your systems.

In forming your Connection System, think of the process in light of the following progression:

1.   Connect with visitor within the first ten minutes relationally (arrival)
2.   Begin your "Seven Touch" process (first two weeks)
3.   Invite returning visitor to an upcoming event (by end of second week)
4.   Connect visitor to one of your Growth Systems (by eighth week)

Of the eighteen systems, the Connection System has the most moving parts. You will continually need to give continual attention to these parts as the system has to adjust and change as the church grows. Why? Because it becomes increasingly more difficult in a larger church with multiple services to spot who is new. By the time your congregation reaches the large church level, visitors have to start self-identifying. Nevertheless, the actual parts of this system remain constant from one size level to the next and these parts can be integrated into new formats as needed.

One more thing! Make sure your visitors are more important than your process. My wife and I once visited a church whose pastor I had coached (poorly, as it turned out) in the Connection System. We were greeted extravagantly at the door, personally escorted to the refreshments, handed great brochures about the church's ministries and led to our seats in the empty main room—where we were left with another visiting family for 15 minutes while the regular attenders of the church had what sounded like a party with each other out in the hall. Smooth process, but a bad system because they forgot the main thing: *people are looking for relationships when they come, not a conveyer belt to the right seat.*

Critical Questions This System Answers:

- Do we have a plan to move people from first time visitors to regular attenders?
- Do we have the right team to connect with new people when they visit?

- What do we do intentionally to connect visitors into a potential relationship with regular attenders within the first ten minutes?

Major Components:

Relationship Opportunities: A list of all the potential relationship openings within the congregation where new people can be directed to connect.

Ten Minute Plan: A plan for how those in charge of greeting people will connect the visitors relationally with others within the first ten minutes of their arrival.

Handout Materials: Materials developed for visitors to answer basic questions about who the church is and reasons for them to take more steps in connecting.

Follow Up Process: A developed plan for how the church will 'touch' the lives of visitors, and continue the connection process past the first visit.

Entry Ministry Opportunities: A list of all the potential entry level ministry opportunities within the congregation where new people can be invited to serve. This addresses the question, "Am I needed?"

Exit Plan for Unhappy Visitors: How leaders will evaluate and approach unhappy visitors to give them permission to move on before they damage the congregation.

Visitor Events: Regularly planned events to which visitors will be invited within the first two weeks of their first visit.

Theology of Partnership: A clarifying statement that defines the beliefs that the church leaders hold on the issue of partner/membership.

Connections Class: The informational process by which new people are invited to learn about the vision and belief of the church before entering into partner/membership.

Hospitality Plan: Hospitality as a sub-system goes well beyond the scope of connection, but for the purposes of this system, this is a plan on how the congregation will use hospitality to connect relationally with new people by meeting their personal needs before, during or after the gathering.

Nursery Strategy: The approach the church will use in its nursery to communicate safety and help to visiting parents.

Coordinator: A recruiting tool for finding the person who oversees this system and for those who will be part of the connection team. This system also requires coordinators running the various components of this system serving in the areas of greeters, ushers, hospitality and follow up.

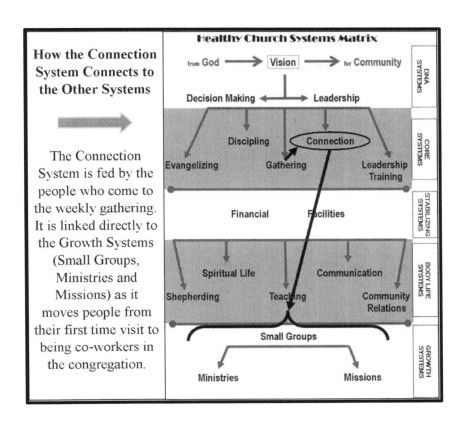

Healthy Church Systems Matrix

How the Connection System Connects to the Other Systems

→

The Connection System is fed by the people who come to the weekly gathering. It is linked directly to the Growth Systems (Small Groups, Ministries and Missions) as it moves people from their first time visit to being co-workers in the congregation.

CONNECTION SYSTEM SURVEY QUESTIONS

Visitor Flow

1 _____ The church averages less than 5 visitors a month.

2 _____ The church averages 5-10 visitors a month.

3 _____ The church averages 3-5 visitors a week.

4 _____ The church averages 6-14 visitors a week.

5 _____ The church averages more than 15 visitors a week.

Visitor Repeats

1 _____ Less than 10% of our visitors return for a second visit.

2 _____ 10% of our visitors return for a second visit.

3 ____   20% of our visitors return for a second visit.

4 ____   25% of our visitors return for a second visit.

5 ____   30% or more of our visitors return for a second visit.

Visitor Retention

1 ____   Of those who return, only 10% remain with the congregation after 12 months.

2 ____   Of those who return, 15% remain with the congregation after 12 months.

3 ____   Of those who return, 20% remain with the congregation after 12 months.

4 ____   Of those who return, 30% remain with the congregation after 12 months.

5 ____   Of those who return, 40%+ remain with the congregation after 12 months.

Attendance Increase

1 ____   Our average gathering attendance over the last three years is flat or has declined.

2 ____   Our average gathering attendance over the last three years has increased less than 5%.

3 ____   Our average gathering attendance over the last three years has increased 10%.

4 ____   Our average gathering attendance over the last three years has increased 10% yearly.

5 ____   Our average gathering attendance over the last three years has increased 20%+ yearly.

Leader

1 ____   Either the pastor or his wife coordinates this system or no one is assigned to oversee it.

2 ____   An untrained volunteer oversees this system.

3 _____   A trained leader over volunteers oversees this system.

4 _____   A dedicated leader leads other leaders and a team in overseeing this system.

5 _____   A dedicated leader mentoring his or her replacement and a team oversees this system.

Total _____ divided by 5 = _____

SYSTEM 8: LEADERSHIP TRAINING

Necessary Outcome: *Future leaders are continually being identified and prepared to lead.*

Introduction

A pastor of a church that had been at over 500 asked me to help him understand why his church was declining. They were culturally relevant in how they sowed the gospel in their community and had many good things happening. As we explored the Healthy Church Systems Matrix together, the pastor recalled how, in the first years of the church, he had filled his house to overflowing with young leaders in whom he was investing. And for reasons of ministry growth and time pressures, one day he simply stopped. That day we met he realized the long-term impact of his decision.

No church can continue to grow without more leaders, because it is having more leaders, not more people, that fuels growth. Having people trained and willing to take charge over vital ministries is essential to healthy church growth. This is the most critical system to focus on in order to grow your church past the 125 level. It is a task that the pastor must give at least 25% of his time. If not, the church will remain a single cell church, with the pastor, instead of the vision, being the focus of the systems of the church. But it is relevant to growing a congregation at all levels.

The central function of this system is to allow the leaders to embrace their biblical function of equipping others for the works of service so that the body of Christ might be built up (Ephesians 4:12). There is an emphasis on on-the-job training, as new leaders are not made in the classroom, but in the field. This is the one system that has to be led by the pastor and the top leadership of the church and not assigned to a coordinator. It is from the leaders of the church that new leaders learn how God wants them to lead.

To develop this system, one has to recognize the tension that you will never have enough leaders. Even if this system is operating at its optimum, a growing church will always need double what it needs right now. A good rule of thumb for every church is, for every ten new leaders you need, double it. And while this may seem an impossible suggestion, it will keep you from thinking too small and hindering your church's ability to increase capacity.

The best place to find good leaders for your church is from among the people who attend, particularly those who have come to the church through conversion and have gone through your Discipling System. These are the ones who should share the DNA of the church's vision and continue to come because they want to accomplish that vision. Growing leaders from among your attenders protects the church from depending on leaders developed by other churches, leaders who may be committed to a different vision for the church. Your attenders may not yet be developed in leadership. Creating a healthy Leadership Training System is critical for the future of your church.

Critical Questions This System Answers:

- Do we actually have a thorough going Leadership Training System?
- How many leaders do we need to develop every year to allow us to enfold more disciples?

Major Components:

Leadership Portrait: The leaders have a developed a comprehensive description of what a mature leader will know and how he or she will behave.

Spotter's List: A developed list of raw talents and abilities to help leaders know what to look for in a potential leader.

Mentoring Plan: A developed process implemented by leaders to train new leaders on the job.

Classroom Training: Supplemental training classes in the areas of spiritual transformation, leadership skills and handling people.

Process Calendaring: What is not on the calendar does not exist. The issue for a church is to find a place for all leadership training units in a repeatable cycle.

Monthly Leadership Meeting: A regular meeting plan bringing all church leaders together, including those in training, for vision renewal, strategy and cross-leadership influence.

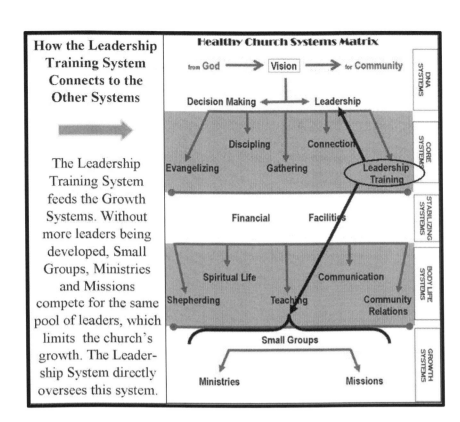

How the Leadership Training System Connects to the Other Systems

The Leadership Training System feeds the Growth Systems. Without more leaders being developed, Small Groups, Ministries and Missions compete for the same pool of leaders, which limits the church's growth. The Leadership System directly oversees this system.

Healthy Church Systems Matrix

LEADERSHIP TRAINING SYSTEM SURVEY QUESTIONS

Process

1 _____   The church has no defined leadership training process.

2 _____   The church has classes in leadership training.

3 _____   The church has a mentoring process or a monthly gathering for leaders as well as leadership training classes.

4 _____   The church has a monthly gathering of leaders and a mentoring process as well as leadership training classes.

5 _____   In addition to a monthly gathering, mentoring and basic leadership classes, the church offers advanced classes in leadership.

Where Leaders Come From

1 _____   90% of our new leaders come from members who transferred into the church from another church.

2 _____   20% of our new leaders are people who came to faith through this church.

3 _____   30% of our new leaders are people who came to faith through this church.

4 _____   40% of our new leaders are people who came to faith through this church.

5 _____   50% of our new leaders are people who came to faith through this church.

Total New Leaders Per Year

1 _____   The church rarely develops and deploys new leaders.

2 _____   The church develops less than 1% of attenders as new leaders every year,

3 _____   The church develops up to 3% of attenders as new leaders every year,

4 _____   The church develops up to 7% of attenders as new leaders every year, which has allowed us to expand our Growth Systems (Small Groups, Ministries, Missions) into new areas.

5 _____   The church develops 10% of attenders as new leaders every year, which allows us to send out leaders to help start a new congregation.

Age of New Leaders

1 _____   More than 60% of new leaders are older than 45.

2 _____   More than 50% of new leaders are older than 45.

3 _____   60% of new leaders are under 45 years old.

4 _____   40% of new leaders are under 35 years old.

5 _____   40% of new leaders are under 25 years old, 10% being in their teens.

1 _____ No one is assigned to oversee leadership training.

2 _____ A volunteer oversees this system.

3 _____ A trained leader oversees this system.

4 _____ The pastor oversees this system.

5 _____ The pastor and his staff oversees this system.

Total _____ divided by 5 = _____

SYSTEM 9: FINANCIAL

Necessary Outcome: *All of the church's income is handled with integrity and used appropriately for the advancement of the Kingdom.*

Introduction

If there is one system that pastors love to hate, it is their Financial System. It is such a necessary one, but the finances of a church can be a source of anger and anxiety in a congregation. It causes anger when people are suspicious and accusatory about how money is being handled. It causes anxiety when there are not enough resources to do the church's ministry the way it could be done if better funded. Many pastors hate the headaches of this system, and therefore allow others to develop and run it. This can lead the church to have two heads—the ministry one led by the pastor and leaders and the financial one led by the financial officers. When these two clash, no one wins. As a pastor, you want to give the right amount of guidance and oversight to this system so that its leaders are on your team.

At the core of developing this system well is the vision of the church. All finances are given to further the work of your congregation's purpose, whether the money is given for your personal support, missions, building purchase or some other ministry focus. Everything that is given allows your church to accomplish its vision. Anyone who is recruited to lead this system has to be convinced of this before he or she signs on. This prevents a tug of war over the church's finances as you go forward.

Your Financial System by nature has two focuses, both of which have to be addressed if you are going to stabilize your church. The first is the *legal aspect* of handling the finances. The second is the *stewardship* side of the church supporting its mission. In other words, you have to make sure you are living within the rules that govern how any non-profit handles its money while at the same time having sufficient money to thrive and grow.

Having a comprehensive Financial System will help your church avoid ever having a problem with the government or with attenders. While most churches fly under the radar with the government, a number of them are actually breaking the law in how they handle their finances. You do not want to tempt God in this matter, so learning and applying the rules is in keeping with Paul's instruction in Romans 13:1. Others are structured in their Financial System in a way that offers opportunities for people to steal. This is a more serious problem than many churches think. Enough churches and religious organizations have had to deal with the sorrowful aftermath of a 'trusted' leader who got caught up in embezzlement. You want to think about how you will protect people from the temptation as best you can.

The goal of this process is to lead you to avoid both of these pitfalls. It is also to save you from the panic that certain seminars for church IRS compliance tend to produce. I have had to talk leaders down from the aftereffects of these seminars, whose presenters took advantage of the lack of knowledge of the attenders to scare them into buying their services!

Equally important is the stewardship side of the system. Most churches struggle with the reality that many of their attenders are poor stewards of what God has given them. Even in times of plenty, these believers tend to practice tipping rather than generosity. Developing this aspect of the system allows the church to disciple people in having a generous heart, becoming better stewards over what God has given them and giving freely to the work of Jesus' kingdom.

Critical Questions This System Answers:

- Are the ones handling the finances people who can always be trusted?
- Are the people in this system on mission with the other leaders so that they work together to move the church forward?
- Does the church have a comprehensive stewardship building process?

Major Components:

Theology of Finances: A clarifying statement of the underlying doctrinal beliefs on the how and why of handling God's money that will be the standard for agenda harmony within the financial team.

Priorities and Decision Makers: The process of defining the church's giving priorities with the top decision makers in order that those who make decisions over all the rest of the budget will know what must be important.

Risk Steps for Growth: Faith steps that the church will determine it is willing to take with its finances in order to grow.

Core Financial Team: Identifying and recruitment of the core members of a complete financial team.

Benevolence: A working benevolence policy to guide those responsible in how to handle this biblical matter.

Credit Cards/Cash Policy: The church's policy on who gets credit cards and when it will hand out cash.

Reimbursement Policy: A reimbursement process that will involve creating a voucher system for staff or responsible ministry leaders before they make a purchase on behalf of the church.

Borrowing Policy: A pre-determining pathway on how to lead the church during times of financial crisis.

Staff Benefits: The goal of any financial decisions for staff in the area of benefits is to bless them as much as the church can within its abilities. Certain benefits are non-taxable and can really help both the staff person and the church.

Government Policies Compliance: Creating or clarifying a number of policies that every church is required by law to have for its financial system.

Stewardship Training Process: How the church will train people to be good stewards over the resources God has given them.

Stewardship Practices: The whys and process the church will adopt to build a stewardship culture throughout the whole congregation.

Process Calendaring: What is not on the calendar does not exist. The issue for a church is to find a place for all stewardship training events in a repeatable cycle.

Budgeting Process: A process that utilizes a budgeting form to help each contributor to itemize and determine their ministry costs in light of how their ministry goals will help the church accomplish its vision.

Coordinator: A recruiting tool for finding the person who oversees this system and helps build the financial team.

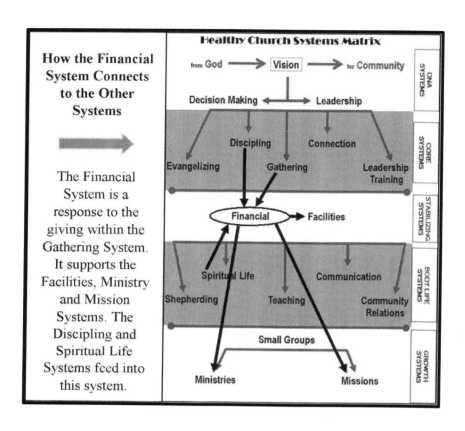

The left panel of the figure reads:

How the Financial System Connects to the Other Systems

The Financial System is a response to the giving within the Gathering System. It supports the Facilities, Ministry and Mission Systems. The Discipling and Spiritual Life Systems feed into this system.

FINANCIAL SYSTEM SURVEY QUESTIONS

Team

1 _____   All finances are handled by the pastor plus 1-2 other people.

2 _____   The church has a team or 2-4 people who oversee the finances, one of whom is the pastor.

3 _____   The church has a financial team that reports to the pastor through a designated leader.

4 _____   The church has a CFO in place who has an experienced team with a written policy manual that guides the church.

5 _____   The church has a CFO with a team, but outsources bookkeeping.

Stability in Giving

0 _____   The church does not track giving by the attenders.

1 _____   25% of the regular attenders give something each month.

2 _____   50% of the regular attenders give something each month.

3 _____   75% of the regular attenders and 10% of the non-regular attenders give something each month, plus there are 1-2 extravagant givers who will respond to any special need of the church.

4 _____   90%+ of the regular attenders and 25% non-regulars give something each month.

5 _____   90%+ of the regular attenders and 40% of the non-regular attenders give something each month.

Support of Missions

1 _____   There is no money in the church budget to support national and international mission agencies, although individuals do designate money for missions.

2 _____   Less than 10% of the church budget is used to support national and international mission agencies.

3 _____   10% of the church budget is used to support national and international mission agencies.

4 _____   15% of the church's budget is for national and international missions, plus money is being set aside for starting a daughter church.

5 _____   A new church has been launched and money is being set aside for another daughter church.

Emergency Funds

1 _____   The church experiences financial difficulties at least 4 out of 12 months.

2 _____   The church has experienced financial difficulties at least 2 out of 12 months.

3 _____   The church has met all its financial obligations without a shortfall for the last 12 months.

4 _____   The leaders have developed an all-church stewardship approach that has increased giving by 10% over the previous year, allowing the church to create an emergency fund capable of covering 1-2 months of the church's budget.

5 _____ The leaders have developed an all-church stewardship approach that has increased giving by 20%+ over the previous year, allowing the church to create an emergency fund capable of covering 3 months of the church's budget, as well as increase the mission giving in the budget by 10%.

Stewardship Training

1 _____ There is no financial/stewardship training process for the attenders.

2 _____ 10% of the attenders have been through stewardship training.

3 _____ 25% of the attenders have been through stewardship training.

4 _____ 50% of the attenders have been through stewardship training and this training is offered to all new attenders as part of their discipleship process.

5 _____ 75% of the attenders have been through stewardship training and this training is expected of all new attenders as part of their discipleship process.

Pastoral Support

1 _____ Currently the church is able to pay the pastor less than 50% of a living wage.

2 _____ The pastor is paid at least 75% of a living wage.

3 _____ The pastor is paid a living wage.

4 _____ The church now is able to hire additional staff full-time.

5 _____ The church now is able to hire additional staff as needed.

Bonus

+1 _____ In addition, there are 5-10 extravagant givers who will respond to any special need of the church.

+2 _____ In addition, there are 11+ extravagant givers who will respond to any special need of the church.

Total _____ divided by 6 = _____

SYSTEM 10: FACILITIES

Necessary Outcome: *Maximized use of the church's facilities so that they are used for the Kingdom all week long.*

Introduction

People have an innate concept of *sacred space*. It can be as small as a chair or as large as a cathedral. It can be a room inside their house, at a building that has been set aside for sacred events or a spot in the great outdoors where they are drawn to worship. When you come to the issue of a Facilities System, you start with the reality that people are looking for this sacred space where they will be able in some way to sense the presence of God. It does not matter if the space is used for different purposes at other times; in their thinking, when the people are present, this area is dedicated to being with God—for themselves as well as others who may be included in their spiritual family. This is why the Facilities System is a theological issue as well as a practical one. No matter what you may believe about the church being made up of the believers wherever they gather, this system asks you to address your congregation's felt need of an appropriate sacred place.

The Facilities System is about having enough space. As churches are started and seek to get established, they have to have space to grow. One church leadership team I worked with told me they were having five visitors weekly. Their meeting space held 140 at best and they were already running over 80% full. I pointed out that five visitors a week translated into 260 potential new attenders per year, which would fill their space twice over. When they realized that they had no more space to enfold people, it dawned on them why new people liked the church, liked the pastoral staff, liked their message, but did not come back!

While space in itself is not a growth mechanism, not having enough space can inhibit a church's ability to increase its capacity for growth. Most churches feel they do not have enough space for their ministries. Many more feel they cannot afford to move into a larger facility because the cost of rental or a mortgage would dominate their finances and prevent them from doing ministry. On the other hand, most churches stop growing because attenders feel their space is too full and that they have no space for new people anyway.

A rule of thumb for not having enough space is: *When you are 80% full, you are full.* While this may not apply to all cultural groups, as some people groups appreciate being crowded together, most people will not long put up with being shoulder to shoulder with people when they are in a sacred space. For you to develop a workable system, you have to accept that when you approach the 70% full mark, you will need to have a plan ready for the next step in making more space available for your congregation.

A final side note—understand that *too much space can defeat you.* Sometimes a church may enter into a phase when its facilities are too large. Maybe the congregation has shrunk or the current rental space is double or more than what you need. Why is this a problem? Because, like being too crowded, being too empty can discourage growth. People may sit too far apart to give them a sense of being connected as a spiritual family. Emptiness can also unwittingly communicate an ineffective witness to the community, lessening attenders' desire to accomplish the vision of the church (an unspoken, "What's the use?"). You will need to come up with a solution to shrink your space to a visually appropriate growth size. Do not just rope off unused areas. Use vision barriers such as screens to box in the space you need at this time.

Critical Questions This System Answers:

- What do we want to use our facilities to accomplish?
- How do we use our facilities (other than on Sundays) for maximum impact?
- Do we have the right team members to care for the facilities we have been given to use?

Major Components:

Space Need: Discovery and planning process about how to fill the church's need for space.

Maintenance: The right team to maintain the facilities is recruited and people are given appropriate access.

Visibility: How the church will deal with the two visibility issues of cleanliness and signage for both attenders and visitors.

Daily Usage: A seven-day plan for usage for the church's space in the areas of ministry, community and income.

Coordinator: A recruiting tool for finding the person who oversees this system and helps build the maintenance team.

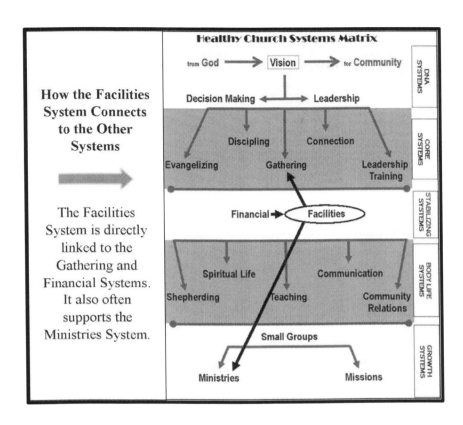

FACILITIES SYSTEM SURVEY QUESTIONS

Costs

1 ____   The cost of the building and additional rental space plus maintenance equals 50%+ of the budget.

2 ____   The cost of the building and additional rental space plus maintenance equals 40% of the budget.

3 ____   The cost of the building and additional rental space plus maintenance equals 35% of the budget.

4 ____   The cost of the building and additional rental space plus maintenance equals 30% of the budget.

5 ____   The cost of the building and additional rental space plus maintenance equals 25% of the budget.

Visibility

1 _____ No sign is allowed for the church to show its presence.

2 _____ Signage is limited to the outside door/wall of the building where we meet, but the church does put out signs on Sundays.

3 _____ The church signage is visible near the road, but lacks clear directional signs inside the building for visitors.

4 _____ The church has both signage near the road and clear directional signs within the building for visitors.

5 _____ The church maintains signage near the road and also off property so that people can know where our building is. Besides directional signs in the building, the church provides a site map for new people.

Usage

1 _____ The church has no comprehensive plan for maximizing building usage.

2 _____ The church has no comprehensive plan for maximizing building use, but it does share its space with another church.

3 _____ The church has a plan to utilize the building three days out of the week for ministry, community or income, but it does share its space with another church.

4 _____ The church has a plan to utilize the building five days out of the week for ministry, community or income, but it does share its space with another church.

5 _____ The church has a plan to utilize the building seven days a week for ministry, community or income, plus it shares its space with more than one other church.

Parking to Attendees Ratio

1 _____ The church has parking space for 1 to 5+ car/seats ratio.

2 _____ The church has parking space for 1 to 4 car/seats ratio.

3 _____ The church has parking space for 1 to 3 car/seats ratio.

4 ____   The church has parking space for 1 to 2 car/seats ratio.

5 ____   The church has parking space for 1 to 1.5 car/seats ratio.

Attendees to Seating Ratio

1 ____   The facility has too much space for the congregation (seating roped off, with the congregation filling less than 50% of the chairs), making the people feel like the room is empty.

2 ____   The facilities have been at or above 80% full for over a year with no firm plan for starting another service or renting more space.

3 ____   The facilities have been 80% full for six months, but the leaders are currently planning to start another service or rent more space.

4 ____   The church has one service that is 80% full, but the leaders run another service(s) which runs under 80%. There is no plan for what to do next.

5 ____   The service(s) has reached 70% full and the leaders already have a plan to either start another service or rent more space

Leader

1 ____   Either the pastor or his wife coordinates this system or no one is assigned to oversee it.

2 ____   An untrained volunteer oversees this system.

3 ____   A trained leader over volunteers oversees this system.

4 ____   A dedicated leader leads other leaders and a team of regular volunteers in overseeing this system.

5 ____   A dedicated leader mentoring his or her replacement and a team of both volunteers and professionals oversees this system.

Total _____ divided by 6 = _____

SYSTEM 11: SHEPHERDING

Necessary Outcome: *Disciples know they are personally cared for and are consistently growing in their faith.*

Introduction

All people need to be shepherded. Shepherding is about making sure the sheep of God's flock are well cared for. But many churches create their Shepherding System in a way that limits the growth and care of the church. For many churches, the majority of the spiritual shepherding is strictly the pastor's domain—this is why many a pastor thinks he is there to take care of each sheep personally! And many pastors accept this as their responsibility because: 1) they like to feel needed; or 2) they are very relational and want to connect in friendship with all attenders; or 3) they never were told that this will limit their ministry.

It is also true that many people like to be shepherded by you, their pastor. They choose to attend a small church specifically because this is important to them. I know of people who felt the church neglected them when they were in the hospital because, although a number of shepherds from the congregation came to minister to them while they were recovering from sickness, their pastor was not one of their visitors. The result of this is that most churches are under 100 in attendance, as this is a common limit of people one pastor can shepherd effectively. When new people come, some of the older attenders leave, feeling that they are no longer connected to the pastor's care.

Think of your congregation's shepherding needs in terms of people and time. In a pastor-centric shepherding model for a church of 100, one or two persons (the pastor and perhaps his wife) provide the largest source of shepherding. Yet the real need is closer to ten people to shepherd 100 people properly. If you have 200 people, then the need goes up by another ten. And so on.

Why ten per hundred? Outside the pastoral staff, few people have unlimited time to give to shepherding others. Yet if your role as the pastor is to equip the congregation for ministry, then your time needs to be given more to developing others than to shepherding everyone personally. When using other leaders to shepherd, you have to pay attention to how much time they have available. Shepherding ten people well is a big job for those who do this ministry. There are exceptions, of course, but ten is a rule of thumb.

The idea of what a shepherd is supposed to do can vary from church to church. Some see it as a deacon ministry. Others see it as personal care that takes place in small group fellowships. No one definition covers all the possibilities, but shepherding can include a variety of ministry: discipling, benevolence, counseling, prayer, visiting the sick and shut-ins and restoration of those caught in sin. Whatever you determine is part of the shepherding role, it is ultimately about people and their relationship to God and each other.

A healthy Shepherding System addresses the issue of increasing capacity. The way to expand the health of the congregation and be in a position to enfold new believers and attenders is to multiply the amount of shepherds your church has. This means identifying and training people to do the ministry of a shepherd, as well as the pastor delegating these responsibilities to such shepherds.

Critical Questions This System Answers:

- Do we have a consistent and growing team of trained shepherds that are personally invested in the care of other attenders?
- Are attenders intentionally being directed into our shepherding process so that they will get their needs met?

Major Components:

Theology of Shepherding: The beliefs that guide your church's practices in the area of shepherding, particularly in the offices of elders and deacons. This includes your biblical view of women's roles in shepherding.

Function and Placement: A defined set of responsibilities for shepherds, plus where the shepherding ministry is integrated into the life of the church.

Shepherd Profile: The characteristics of those who the church selects for the shepherding role.

Training Process: When and how each shepherd will be trained in the necessary skills to make them effective for this ministry.

Shepherd's Report Form: A form that will pass on vital information to the pastoral staff concerning the congregation's spiritual and personal needs. **Prayer Team:** The prayer approach that the church will follow to meet needs—sickness, fears, losses, etc.—of people.

Coordinator: A recruiting tool for finding the person who oversees this system and helps build the shepherding team.

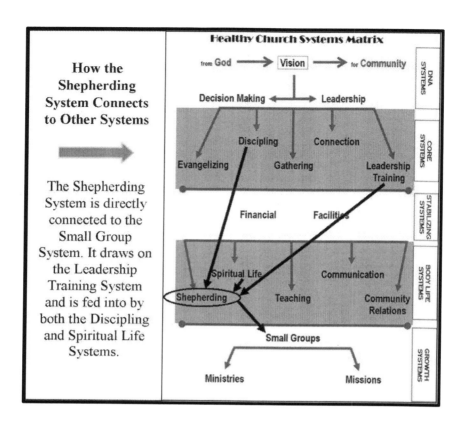

SHEPHERDING SYSTEM SURVEY QUESTIONS

Training

1 _____ The church provides no training process for those who serve as spiritual shepherds.

2 _____ The church provides basic training to spiritual shepherds, but has no assignment pathway to connect them with specific attenders.

3 _____ The church provides basic training to spiritual shepherds and assigns them to specific attenders to oversee.

4 _____ The church provides basic training to spiritual shepherds and assigns them to a specific ministry to care for the people who are part of that ministry.

5 _____ The church provides both training and mentoring for spiritual shepherds to prepare them for their work and assigns them to a specific ministry.

Proportion of Shepherds to Attenders

1 _____   1 shepherd for over 40 people

2 _____   1 shepherd for up to 40 people

3 _____   1 shepherd for up to 30 people

4 _____   1 shepherd for up to 20 people

5 _____   1 shepherd for up to 15 people

Pathway to Discipleship

1 _____   Shepherds are not expected to provide any specific discipling guidance.

3 _____   Shepherds provide one-on-one discipling for people under their care.

5 _____   Shepherds guide people under their care through the church's discipling process.

Leader

1 _____   Either the pastor or his wife coordinates this system or no one is assigned to oversee it.

2 _____   An untrained volunteer oversees this system.

3 _____   A trained leader over volunteers oversees this system.

4 _____   A dedicated leader leads other leaders and a team in overseeing this system.

5 _____   A dedicated leader mentoring his or her replacement and a team oversees this system.

Bonus

+1 _____   New people are assigned to a shepherd or shepherding ministry within the first month.

Total _____ divided by 4 = _____

SYSTEM 12: SPIRITUAL LIFE

Necessary Outcome: *Disciples demonstrate passion for God and His Kingdom.*

Introduction

This system should be considered the life pulse of the church, even above its vision. It is how people come to know God and respond to His leading over the congregation. While it is included as one of the Body Life Systems, Spiritual Life is foundational for all the systems, even the church's Vision. When leaders pay tireless attention to this system, it is what makes the church alive. This system is more than about increasing capacity. Without a healthy spiritual life system, the church will eventually crack and splinter when spiritual warfare gets hot and people's sin is exposed.

Often churches assume that spiritual life is not a system and that it will happen naturally. While there is much truth to this belief, the function of a Spiritual Life System is to make sure the church is engaged regularly in spiritual disciplines that will encourage people to pursue deeper intimacy with God. Times of prayer, fasting and other such activities cannot be only spontaneous; they need to be planned and initiated in appropriate settings within the body life of the church. Also, knowing how to restore those caught in sin is a critical part of this system. Essentially, a healthy spiritual life system is about the intentional ways you will engage with God to enhance spiritual life in your attenders.

Too many churches have blown up because this system has been assumed instead of intentionally developed. The toughest sights I have observed in ministry are in churches where seemingly the spiritual life of the congregation is going quite well until a crisis appears. The crisis then exposes the lack of deep spiritual intimacy with God among those who attend and numerous people end up wounded or leaving. I have seen churches of 500 people end up as two small churches of 100 with the other 300 wandering between churches or going nowhere. Often these disasters were over issues of small consequence made larger because of the neglect of spiritual maturation of the congregation. Seeking to develop a spiritual life system then is almost too late in the game. That is why this system is as foundational to the ongoing life of the congregation as any other body life system.

One pastor I know who took this system seriously began to focus on where he would include transformational training in his congregation. The church had been introduced to the basic teaching about pursuing intimacy with God, but had not included the disciplines of intimacy into the ongoing life of their faith community. With his leading, these transformational disciplines were integrated into their Small Group System. He reported that as the small group attenders became more engaged with pursuing intimacy with God through these disciplines, his counseling load dropped significantly. This is just one example of why it is important to be intentional about your Spiritual Life System.

Critical Questions This System Answers:

- Are people showing outward signs and verbal affirmations of true spiritual change?
- Do we know how to spot the difference between the outward conformity model and transformational model of spiritual life?

Major Components:

Theology of Spiritual Life: The beliefs that guide your church's practices in the area of spiritual life, particularly in the areas of confession, repentance, reconciliation and restoration.

Spiritual Life Expectations: The practices church leaders are expected to do in their own spiritual life.

Training Process: How attenders are trained in spiritual transformation.

Restoration Process: A practical process by which people who fall into sin are restored in their walk with God and with the congregation.

Theology and Practice of Communion: How and why this congregation practices communion the way it does.

Place and Timing of Spiritual Disciplines: How and when the congregation will be led to practice various spiritual disciplines pertinent to the life of the church.

Coordinator: A recruiting tool for finding the person who oversees this system and helps build the spiritual life team.

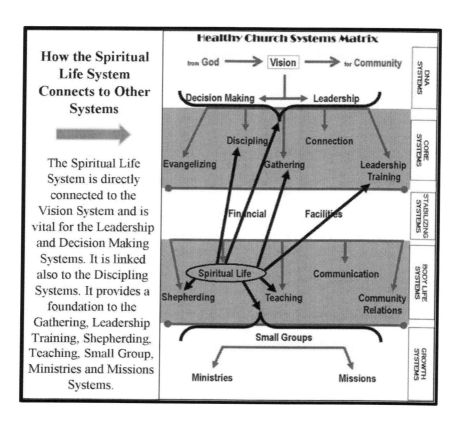

SPIRITUAL LIFE SYSTEM SURVEY QUESTIONS

Practiced Regularly

1 _____ The church regularly practices worship and Bible study.

3 _____ Besides worship and Bible Study, the church has a regularly scheduled prayer time together.

5 _____ Besides worship, Bible study and a regular prayer time, the church teaches intimacy with God through spiritual disciplines.

Growth of Prayer Involvement

1 _____ The church has no way of measuring how many attenders are involved in prayer for the people and ministry of the church.

2 _____ 10% of the attenders participate in at some form of prayer time in the life of the church.

3 ____   25% of the attenders participate in at some form of prayer time in the life of the church.

4 ____   50% of the attenders participate in at some form of prayer time in the life of the church.

5 ____   75% of the attenders participate in at some form of prayer time in the life of the church.

Counseling Load

1 ____   The church leaders see 1 out of 4 attenders or more sometime during the year for more than one session of counseling (couples count as two).

2 ____   The church leaders see 1 out of 5 attenders sometime during the year for more than one session of counseling (couples count as two).

3 ____   The church leaders see 1 out of 8 attenders sometime during the year for more than one session of counseling (couples count as two).

4 ____   The church leaders see 1 out of 10 attenders sometime during the year for more than one session of counseling (couples count as two).

5 ____   The church leaders see 1 out of 15 attenders or less sometime during the year for more than one session of counseling (couples count as two).

Restoration Process

1 ____   The church has never practiced a restoration process with people who fall into sin.

3 ____   The only restoration process the church has had has been done by the pastor.

3 ____   The restoration process in the church is led by the pastor and the leaders only.

4 ____   The pastor has trained a lay team to lead in the restoration process.

5 ____	The majority of the restoration processes are initiated by lay people in the church, either through the shepherds or through the leaders of small groups.

Leader

1 ____	Either the pastor or his wife coordinates this system or no one is assigned to oversee it.
2 ____	An untrained volunteer oversees this system.
3 ____	A trained leader over volunteers oversees this system.
4 ____	A dedicated leader leads other leaders and a team in overseeing this system.
5 ____	A dedicated leader mentoring his or her replacement and a team oversees this system.

Bonus

+1 ____	The church engages in a yearly special time/retreat of spiritual renewal through spiritual practices apart from preaching.
+1 ____	The church has a grace model of transformational training process.
+3 ____	The church has a clear grace model of transformational training process through which over 50% of the attenders have gone.

Total _____ divided by 5 = _____

SYSTEM 13: TEACHING

Necessary Outcome: *Disciples are becoming measurably more knowledgeable of God and the Word.*

Introduction

All pastors know about teaching. If you have spent any time in school preparing for ministry, you have your notebooks—possibly your head—full of all kinds of biblical information. Teaching, along with preaching, forms the backbone of our calling—to make disciples of all nations by *teaching* them to obey everything Jesus taught us. Today, however, many churches assume too much about the effectiveness of their Teaching System.

One question I continually ask new church pastors is, "Where is the congregation exposed to systematic biblical teaching?" One pastor told me it was in their small groups. When I pressed him, he recognized that it was application of the Scripture on which the people focused and not on gaining doctrinal or biblical knowledge. While I am all for how-to-live-the-faith-life application, I know that your church will suffer in time if there is a lack of a grasp of the Bible and sound doctrine. For example, any day a member of a quasi-Christian cult can show up at the door of your people. Besides shutting the door in their faces, what case are they able to make for their faith outside of saying: "This is what my church/pastor believes."? Clearly they need more biblical knowledge than they will learn in the total time of 26 hours a year (that is 30 minutes a sermon times 52 weeks)—assuming they do not miss a Sunday!

In the past, Sunday School offered for many churches its main diet of biblical training. Most newer churches have abandoned Sunday School, but have not effectively replaced it. Teaching is a critical component of all healthy churches, yet many churches have no clear systematic approach to teaching. It can happen in small groups, large group gathering, Sunday schools, children's programs, discipleship groups, etc. But often these teachings are disconnected and the teachers themselves are not in agreement about certain important issues, creating confusion in the congregation.

The function of this system is not to require you to reinstate Sunday School but to help you establish a firm foundation for your people to be able to feed themselves biblically. This system is about the how, what and where people are exposed to the breath of the truths of Scripture. It challenges you to integrate doctrinal training into the life of the congregation. It also leads you to protect your congregation by pre-determining your response to false doctrine that may plague your church as it sneaks in through a popular teacher or a dysfunctional leader who believes he or she has new and better insight into the truths of God.

This system goes further, asking you to strategize biblical training at all age levels—children, teens, adults. Those who are trained in solid biblical truths as children and teens will emerge into young adulthood better prepared for the spiritual tests they will face. When the Teaching System is done well, your church will gain a proper foundation upon which to build its future ministry.

Critical Questions This System Answers:

- Do we have an agreed upon doctrinal statement that captures what we believe about God and guides the teaching in our fellowship?
- Where are we offering complete training in biblical and doctrinal truths?

Major Components:

Theological Parameters: A clear and concise doctrinal statement that will define the boundaries of all teaching that happens in your fellowship.

Theological Agreement Requirement for Teachers: A clear agreement of the level of alignment with the church's doctrinal statement that people who teach at your church must have.

Teacher's Training Process: How and who will be trained up within the church as teachers.

Teacher's Covenant: A common covenant that gives all teachers a point of reference for the boundaries of the church's doctrine and expectations.

Core Doctrinal Training: A plan for what, how, when and where the church's doctrinal beliefs will be taught to the attenders.

Plan for Dealing with False Doctrine: A process for how your church will deal with false teaching and those that promote it within your fellowship.

Core Biblical Knowledge for Teens, Adults and Children: A clear understanding of what constitutes indispensable Bible knowledge that will be taught for each age group.

Process Calendaring: What is not on the calendar does not exist. The issue of calendaring is to find a place for all biblical teaching units in a repeatable cycle.

Coordinator: A recruiting tool for finding the person who oversees this system and helps build the teaching team.

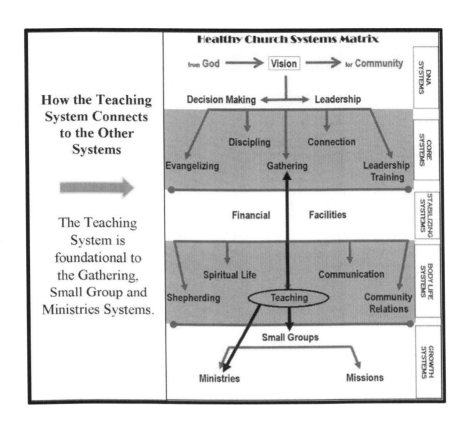

TEACHING SYSTEM SURVEY QUESTIONS

Purpose and Focus

1 ____   The church has no Bible/doctrinal teaching plan, allowing leaders to teach whatever they choose.

2 ____   The church follows a purchased curriculum, but has no internal Bible/doctrinal teaching plan, so the curriculum has not been evaluated to see if it meets the church's needs.

3 ____   The church has a Bible/doctrinal teaching plan and purchases curriculum that fits its needs.

4 ____   The church has a Bible/doctrinal teaching plan and has a team that creates curriculum for its needs.

5 ____   The church has a Bible/Doctrinal teaching plan that offers the equivalent of a college level certificate.

Doctrinal Alignment

1 _____   The church has no doctrinal requirement for teachers.

3 _____   The church has a doctrinal statement that teachers are expected to follow, although not all adhere to it.

5 _____   The church has a doctrinal statement that requires signed agreement from potential teachers before they can teach.

Percentage of Congregation under Teaching

1 _____   The church does not offer any classes in the area of biblical and doctrinal knowledge beyond teaching from the pulpit.

2 _____   10% of the attenders are under teaching offered by the church.

3 _____   25% of the attenders are under teaching offered by the church.

4 _____   50% of the attenders are under teaching offered by the church.

5 _____   60%+ of the attenders are under teaching offered by the church.

Leader

1 _____   Either the pastor or his wife coordinates this system or no one is assigned to oversee it.

2 _____   An untrained volunteer oversees this system.

3 _____   A trained leader over volunteers oversees this system.

4 _____   A dedicated leader leads other leaders and a team in overseeing this system.

5 _____   A dedicated leader mentoring his or her replacement and a team oversees this system.

Bonus

+1 _____   The church is continually training quality teachers so that the church is able increase its teaching ministry.

+1 _____   The church has developed a comprehensive children's Bible/doctrinal training curriculum.

Total _____ divided by 4 = _____

System 14: Communication

Necessary Outcome: *Disciples are increasingly supportive of the leaders because they are informed about what is going on and what decisions are being made for the church.*

Introduction

A man once questioned me about an event that was happening two days later, claiming he had not heard anything about it until that day. The truth was, he had received three emails and a personal phone call announcing the event in the previous months. Announcement had happened. What had not happened was *communication*. And communication is so very important because when people do not know or understand what is going on, they come to their own answers and their conclusions often do not reflect well on your ministry.

People frequently do not hear what you think you have communicated! This is why so many messages you send out in church never seem to make the impact you expected. To have a healthy Communication System, you have to pay attention to how people receive and translate information. At its most basic level, communication takes place when the thought picture in your head comes out of your mind through spoken or written words or through visuals and that same thought picture enters into the mind of others through their eyes or ears reproduced exactly like it was in yours.

However, to develop a Communication System, you have to remember that people are almost always either receiving or sending messages. In fact, in our culture, people are overloaded with messages, so they tend to filter out or check out at times when you are trying to communicate. Unless you can break into their communication loop, your messages are more likely to not be recorded in their memory.

In a growing church, the ability to understand and to make accessible communication is critical to its ability to increase capacity. Somewhere between the 125 and the 250 level, you lose the ability to personally "catch up" every person who missed an important communication. Nor can you afford the costs of miscommunication, because when people do not "hear" after the congregation passes the 250 level, the greater the probability the church's growth will be adversely affected. People will begin to feel disconnected from what is going on. They will also miss essential opportunities to participate in the life of the body.

To develop this system, you need to grasp the basic rudiments of Communication Theory, which is about how people receive and hear messages. The most important of these guidelines is that people remember what they *both* see and hear rather than what they *either* see or hear. The combination of communication practices increases the probability that people "hear."

Also recognize that communication is a two-way street. For your Communication System to work well you have to finish the loop—you need feedback to know that people have heard. One aspect of developing this system is to construct and monitor a method that attenders can use to get information to you and the leaders. You will never get 100%, but find a feedback pathway that attracts the majority to respond. (An example would be a response card to be turned in immediately upon people hearing the message.) Done well, this last piece can go a long way to gain credibility for you—people want to know they are heard at the same level as they are expected to hear.

Critical Questions This System Answers:

- Are we seeing people consistently respond to our communications in the way we expect them to?
- Are we hearing back from the attenders things we need to know?

Major Components:

How Attenders Hear: Clarification on how the people in your church hears messages.

Philosophy of Public Announcements: A plan for breaking into the emotional communication loop of the attenders.

Church Spokespersons: Decision on who are the best persons to represent the congregation to the community and the other churches in your area.

Communication Tools: The tools and methods your church will use to communicate within the congregation and to the community in which the church is.

Coordinator: A recruiting tool for finding the person who oversees this system and helps build the communication team.

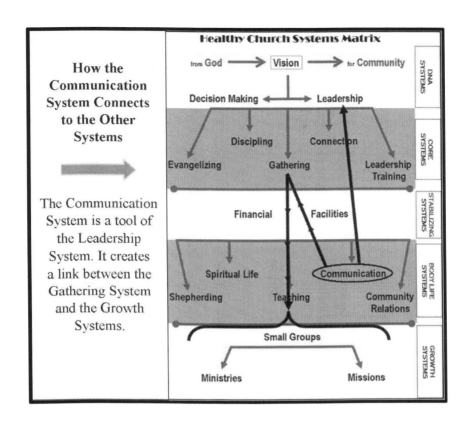

COMMUNICATION SYSTEM SURVEY QUESTIONS

Highest Communication Form

1 _____   Communication verbal.

3 _____   Communication visual.

5 _____   Communication interactive with a feedback loop from the congregation.

Communication Process

1 _____   A worship service verbal announcement system.

2 _____   A mailing/phoning system.

3 _____   An email system.

4 _____   A Website/Facebook system.

5 _____   A texting/tweeting system.

Congregational Feedback

1 _____   There is no feedback loop for people in the church to let the leaders know what they are thinking outside of sharing verbally their thoughts when with a leader.

2 _____   People are encouraged verbally by the leaders to fill out a card on their thoughts or ideas at least once a month during a service.

4 _____   People are encouraged verbally to give feedback to the leaders through the website or Facebook, a card or a text at least once a month.

3 _____   People are encouraged verbally by the leaders to give feedback through the website, Facebook, a card or through a text weekly during a service.

5 _____   The leaders meet monthly with groups of people from the church or send texts out to people to gather information and feedback.

Updating Communication Tools

1 _____   The church seldom updates its website and other visual communication tools.

3 _____   The website and other visual communication tools are updated monthly.

5 _____   The website and other visual communication tools are updated weekly.

Increased Participation in Valued Events (Significant Corporate Outreach or Worship)

1 _____   There has been no significant percentage of increase in attendance at valued events in the last 12 months.

3 _____   The church has seen an increase of participation in valued events by up to 5%.

3 _____   The church has seen an increase of participation in valued events by up to 10%.

4 _____	The church has seen an increase of participation in valued events by up to 15%.
5 _____	The church has seen an increase of participation in valued events by up to 30%.

Leader

1 _____	Either the pastor or his wife coordinates this system or no one is assigned to oversee it.
2 _____	An untrained volunteer oversees this system.
3 _____	A trained leader over volunteers oversees this system.
4 _____	A dedicated leader leads other leaders and a team in overseeing this system.
5 _____	A dedicated leader mentoring his or her replacement and a team oversees this system.

Bonus

+1 _____	The church has a smart phone communication plan.
+1 _____	The church creates its own video for communication.
+1 _____	The pastor has a daily blog that keeps the congregation encouraged and informed.

Total _____ divided by 6 = _____

SYSTEM 15: COMMUNITY RELATIONS

Necessary Outcome: *The people of our community both know we are here and benefit from our ministry to them.*

Introduction

The critical question every church has to ask itself is, "If our church closed its doors today, would anyone notice? Would anyone miss us?" Being salt and light in a community means more than having a place to meet and wonderful programs within the building. It means *community presence and engagement*. For many churches, this translates as the pastor is to be engaged with other ministers at least, and perhaps a joint public service or a public prayer offered at some meeting. This falls far short of a healthy Community Relations System.

Community relations helps your church to impact its community. When working with one church planting pastor, I told him he needed to raise his church's visibility in their community. He scoffed because he thought I meant 'sending out a mailer.' I explained that I was encouraging his church to discover a need in the community and fill it. If they did this, his church would begin to gain a reputation within the community and people would not only know they were there, they possibly would begin to see the church as a positive good instead of something to be ignored. For churches that are looking to attract people who do not like religion, a good Community Relations System can lead to the good deeds that cause people to glorify God.

The Community Relations System involves several practices that too many churches do not actually do. In fact, even churches that at one time practiced healthy community relations have moved away from that pursuit for faulty theological reasons or just plain neglect. This system depends on intentionality. You have to approach it with the idea that it is important. You have to go out and develop relationships with key people in the community. You have to find your voice in the community in terms of ministry and influence. It leads you to connect properly with other churches in the community for shared concerns and impact for the gospel.

This system has much in common with the Vision of your church. Some of the methods that are used to develop this system are drawn from that system. Without a robust Community Relations System, your church is not prepared to meet known needs within the community, much less to step into the gap of emergencies that pop up in your community after personal or physical tragedies.

Critical Questions This System Answers:

- If we closed our doors tomorrow, what difference would it make to the community around us?
- What are we prepared to do to proclaim the gospel through our good deeds?

Major Components:

Relationship: Identifying and engaging with key leaders in the community so they can become acquainted with you and your leaders in a purposeful way.

Discovery Process: The pathway by which the Spirit gives you insight into the community, your co-workers and your apostolic passion. From these three discoveries you will come to know how your congregation will engage with the community in ministry and service.

Serving Plan: A defined approach to understanding what your community needs that your congregation can supply.

Emergency Response Plan: A crisis response plan for emergencies in your community.

Connection with Local Churches: How your church will partner—and at what level—with the other churches in town.

Coordinator: A recruiting tool for finding the person who oversees this system and helps build the community relations team.

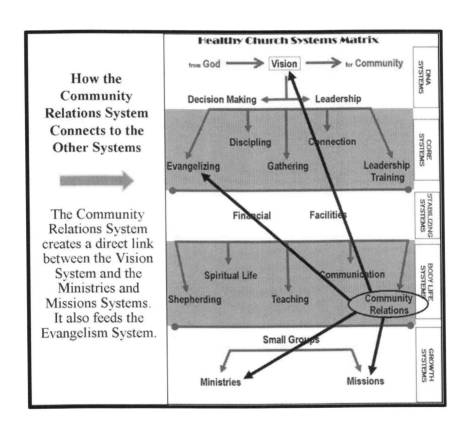

Alignment of Ministries and Community

1 _____   Less than 5% of our ministries are focused on people outside the church.

2 _____   Up to 10% of our ministries are focused on people outside the church.

3 _____   Up to 15% of our ministries are focused on people outside the church.

4 _____   Up to 25% of our ministries are focused on people outside the church.

5 _____   More than 25% of our ministries are focused on people outside the church.

Cooperation with Other Local Churches

1 _____   The pastor and leaders of the church have no involvement with other local churches.

2 _____   The pastor and leaders meet casually with other local church pastors and leaders periodically.

3 _____   The pastor and leaders meet monthly with other church local pastors and leaders.

4 _____   The pastor and other church leaders meet weekly with other local church pastors/leaders for prayer and worship

5 _____   The pastor and leaders have involved the church in collaborative ministries with other churches.

Community Leaders

1 _____   The pastor knows and is known by less than 5 community leaders outside the church body by name.

2 _____   The pastor knows and is known by more than 5 community leaders outside the church body by name.

3 _____   The pastor and church know and are known by more than 10 community leaders outside the church body by name.

5 _____   The pastor and leaders are personally asked by different community leaders to participate in community events at least three times a year.

5 _____   The pastor and leaders spend time with community leaders exploring how the church can help the community monthly.

Response to Community Needs

1 _____   The church has no plan for helping the community when needs arise.

2 _____   The church asks for volunteers to respond to community needs when asked.

3 _____   The church sends volunteers to respond to community needs without being asked whenever the church leaders become aware of a need.

4 _____   The church has a team trained and ready to respond to community needs.

5 _____   The church has multiple teams trained and ready to respond to community needs.

Community Building Usage

1 _____   The church building is never used by any outside group from the community.

2 _____   The church building is used by the community 1-2 times a year when requested.

3 _____   A group within the community uses the church building at least monthly upon request.

4 _____   Multiple groups within the community use the church building weekly upon request.

5 _____   The church leaders have a Seven-Day plan for community usage of the building and actively recruits groups for this purpose.

Leader

1 _____   Either the pastor or his wife coordinates this system or no one is assigned to oversee it.

2 ____	An untrained volunteer oversees this system.
3 ____	A trained leader over volunteers oversees this system.
4 ____	A dedicated leader leads other leaders and a team in overseeing this system.
5 ____	A dedicated leader mentoring his or her replacement and a team oversees this system.

Bonus

+1 ____	The leaders of the church carried out a community discovery process within the last two years.

Total _____ divided by 6 = _____

SYSTEM 16: SMALL GROUPS

Necessary Outcome: *All attenders become part of a small group to build up each other in the faith.*

Introduction

I grew up in church with the Small Groups system called Sunday School. If you have ever observed Sunday School as practiced in many churches, one fact that jumps out at you is that once an adult person joins a class, he, she or they will be with the people in that class either until death or Jesus returns! Sunday School is not the only Small Groups System churches have used, but what can be learned from them is that people bond more deeply with others in the church when they belong to some smaller unit in the large church. Small Groups is the first of the Growth Systems, because it helps the congregation retain people through deepening relationships. People stick to the church because they know they are loved. Having a healthy and well-structured Small Groups System offers you a huge opportunity to increase your church's capacity to absorb new people.

Small groups do vary in purpose and function in churches. Some churches have more than one Small Groups System. Some have been around for many years— Sunday School as noted. Some are recent developments and are still morphing. The starting point for any church is to answer the question, "Do we have a clear idea why we have small groups?" What kind of small groups do you want for your church?

Small groups can fulfill a number of important functions in your church—evangelism, discipleship, prayer, Bible study, missions—but they will only do what you develop and oversee them to do. Shaping the right Small Groups System flows first from your vision from God for the community, then secondly from the purpose of small groups in your fellowship.

A rule of thumb for an *unhealthy* Small Groups System is that the shelf life of any small group will be about eighteen months. After that it either comes to an end or, more likely, it has lost all its original members. The exception to this rule of thumb is a Small Groups System that is totally friendship-based in nature. This is not necessarily a good thing, but it does provide the glue to hold a small group together longer than normal. To move beyond the eighteen month limit is your goal in developing this system.

One important way this happens is for your church to develop a leadership skeleton based on some form of the 'Jethro Model.' Giving small group leaders continual mentoring is what it takes to move groups from the unhealthy to the healthy column. It also helps promote ongoing potential leader identification and development. And it provides your coordinator with a team to give clear oversight that will prevent your small groups from drifting away from their purpose.

Critical Questions This System Answers:

- Do we have a clear idea why we have small groups?
- Do we know what our small groups are to do for the health and growth of the church?
- Are the groups actually achieving this goal?

Major Components:

Group Types: A clear understanding of what kind of groups your church will have and what they will do for the church.

Group Function: A plan for small groups to provide communion, community and mission.

Lesson Material Selection: Guidelines over how lesson materials are chosen.

Entry Pathway: Pathway for people to move from the main gathering into a small group.

Leadership Skeleton: A leadership plan for the church's small groups.

Leadership Basic Training: Basic training process for new leaders using the classroom and on-the-job apprenticeship

Leadership Advanced Training: Advanced training for small group leaders in biblical knowledge, people skills and shepherding.

Coordinator: A recruiting tool for finding the person who oversees this system and helps build the small groups team.

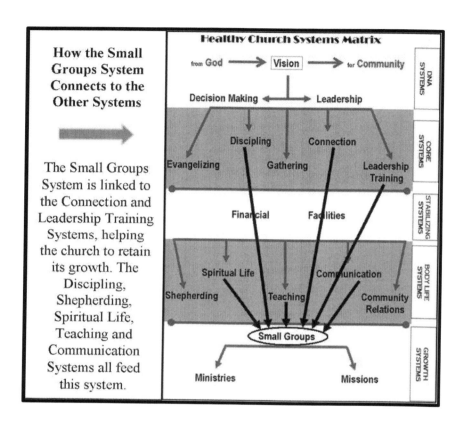

SMALL GROUPS SYSTEM SURVEY QUESTIONS

Participation

1 _____   The church has sporadic groups of various kinds operating, with less than 10% of the attenders participating.

2 _____   The church has regular small groups of various kinds operating, with less than 35% of the attenders participating.

3 _____   The church has a system of small groups, with less than 35% of the attenders participating.

| 4 ____ | The church has a system of small groups, with up to 60% of the attenders participating. |
| 5 ____ | The church has a system of small groups, with more than 80% of the attenders participating. |

Oversight

1 ____	There is no oversight leader over the small groups.
2 ____	A leader is in charge of maintaining the Small Groups System.
3 ____	The leader of small groups has implemented quality standards for the small groups and is regularly meeting with the leaders to train and check standards.
4 ____	Leaders of 50, under a leader of 100, attend in rotation each small group in order to maintain the quality of each.
5 ____	The church has more than one leader of 100 in place, who train and mentor the leaders of the Small Groups System.

Training

1 ____	The church has no training process for small group leaders. Over 80% of the small group leaders transferred in from a previous church.
2 ____	The church has a basic classroom training program for new small groups leaders. 25% of new leaders came to faith in the church.
3 ____	The church has a basic classroom training program for new small groups leaders. 35% of new leaders came to faith in the church.
4 ____	The church has a basic and advanced classroom training program for new small groups leaders. 50% of new leaders came to faith in the church.
5 ____	The church has a basic and advanced classroom training program for new small groups leaders. 60% or more of new leaders came to faith in the church.

Leader

| 1 ____ | Either the pastor or his wife coordinates this system or no one is assigned to oversee it. |

2 ____	An untrained volunteer oversees this system.
3 ____	A trained leader over volunteers oversees this system.
4 ____	A dedicated leader leads other leaders and a team in overseeing this system.
5 ____	A dedicated leader mentoring his or her replacement and a team oversees this system.

Bonus

+2 ____	The church practices on-the-job mentoring for small group apprentices.

Total _____ divided by 4 = _____

SYSTEM 17: MINISTRIES

Necessary Outcome: *All attenders find a place in a healthy ministry.*

Introduction

Ministries are the second growth engine of the church. Being involved in significant ministries encourages attenders to grow in their faith by giving themselves to others. It answers the question, "Am I needed?" Ministries also draw people into deeper relationships so they will find their place in the Kingdom and your church. This will give your church more options to grow ministries and include more people, increasing your capacity.

Many ministries typically grow up over the life cycle of a church. In a healthy church, ministries come from a desire to accomplish the vision God has given the church. Ministries range from helping people in the church to grow in their walk with God to reaching into the lives of people outside the church. There is no set list of ministries that any one church should have, although many churches have ministries to set groups, such as children, teens and senior adults. But to have a robust church, you will continually need to start and then evaluate ministries in light of how they help your church accomplish the vision God has given you. Neglecting this will create the burden on too many non-aligned ministries eating up time and financial resources that do not move the church forward in its mission.

As you begin building ministries in your church, you need to follow this dictum: *Never start a new ministry without first having a leader.* People who attend your church will have all kinds of ministries they would like to see and may strongly urge you as pastor to implement. Do not fall into the pastor-centric trap of starting something that no one is willing to sustain or you will experience either ministry failure that will be blamed on you or you will find all your time used up trying to keep all the supposedly important ministries functioning.

A second dictum you need to follow if you are just starting a church is: *Do a few things well that will build the church instead of trying to do everything.* Do not start out trying to offer the menu of ministry choices a decentralized church would be able to provide, as I saw in one church I worked with. People there were dying on the vine because of the demands made on their time, with some people having to do two or three ministries each. Doing a few things well will allow you to focus your energies and establish a foundation for the future as those ministered to through what you are doing connect deeply with your fledgling congregation. Remember that your ministries are just one of the Growth Systems to build your church. So do not overwhelm your people with too many choices and too many demands for service at the start.

However, the flip side of this is if you want to increase capacity and grow the congregation further, you have to anticipate and initiate. That means that, from your priority list, you will prepare and launch new ministries ahead of the need. Want young families to attend, but have no children's program? In faith prepare to start such a ministry. One church I knew started a nursery even though they did not have one baby among them. The week after they launched their 'unneeded' nursery, several mothers with babies showed up. Anticipating and initiating ministries is a way of expanding your answer to the question, "Am I wanted?"

Critical Questions This System Answers:

- Do our current ministries reflect the vision and direction of our church?
- Do our ministries lead people to a Kingdom mentality or do they encourage self-focus?
- Do we encourage people to do ministry outside the walls of the building without insisting they do ministry inside as well?

Major Components:

Essential Ministry List: A list of the essential ministries that will help your church accomplish its vision, even if you are not in the position to launch them at this moment.

Ministry Balance Evaluation: Balancing the percentage of outward-focused ministries your church offers with the inward-focused ones.

Ministry Development Forms: Tools to evaluate new and existing ministries to align them with the church's vision.

Theology of Ministers: Beliefs about people's calling to be equipped for the work of ministry that guide the recruiting and development of ministers (note: in Jesus' kingdom, people are not asked to volunteer, but to serve).

Recruiting Strategy: A plan for your church's ongoing recruiting strategy.

Job Descriptions: A job description for every ministry position.

Minister's Support Process: The process by which your church retains ministers through appropriate gratitude and respect.

Coordinator: A recruiting tool for finding the person who oversees this system and helps build the ministries team.

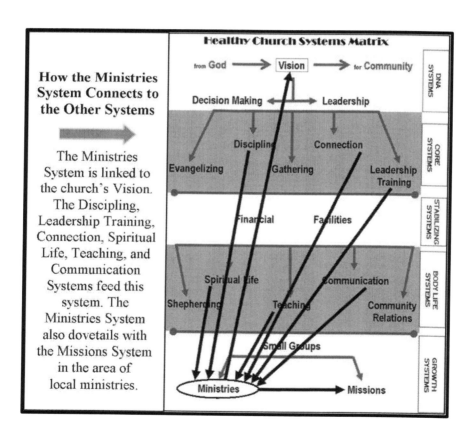

MINISTRIES SYSTEM SURVEY QUESTIONS

Focus

1 _____   Less than 5% of our ministries are focused on people outside the church.

2 _____   Up to 10% of our ministries are focused on people outside the church.

3 _____   From 11-15% of our ministries are focused on people outside the church.

4 _____   From 16-25% of our ministries are focused on people outside the church.

5 _____   More than 26% of our ministries are focused on people outside the church.

Participation

1 _____   Less than 25% of the regular attenders are connected to any ministry.

2 _____   Up to 35% of the regular attenders are connected to one of the ministries.

3 _____   Up to 50% of the regular attenders are connected to one of the ministries.

4 _____   Up to 75% of the regular attenders are connected to one of the ministries.

5 _____   Over 75% of the regular attenders are connected to one of the ministries.

Alignment

1 _____   The leaders have never evaluated how well the ministries align with the vision.

2 _____   An evaluation shows that 50% of the ministries are in alignment with the vision.

3 _____   An evaluation shows that 75% of the ministries are in alignment with the vision.

4 _____   An evaluation shows that 90% of the ministries are in alignment with the vision.

5 _____   An evaluation shows that 100% of the ministries are in alignment with the vision.

Expanding Ministries

1 _____   The church does not have enough leaders to run critical ministries, so more than half of the leaders have two or more ministry responsibilities.

2 _____   The church does not have enough leaders to run critical ministries, so more than 25% of the leaders have two or more ministry responsibilities.

3 _____   The church has enough leaders to equal its current need so that no one has to have more than one ministry responsibility.

4 _____   The church has enough leaders to allow it to start up to 4 new ministries a year

5 _____   The church has enough leaders to allow it to start more than 5 new ministries a year.

Leader

1 _____   Either the pastor or his wife coordinates this system or no one is assigned to oversee it.

2 _____   An untrained volunteer oversees this system.

3 _____   A trained leader over volunteers oversees this system.

4 _____   A dedicated leader leads other leaders and a team in overseeing this system.

5 _____   A dedicated leader mentoring his or her replacement and a team oversees this system.

Bonus

+2 _____   The church leaders do a yearly evaluation of all ministries.

Total _____ divided by 5 = _____

SYSTEM 18: MISSIONS

Necessary Outcome: *The church reflects a demonstrative involvement in all phases of the Acts 1:8 mission.*

Introduction

Mission is the outworking of our faith. It is the last system to be mentioned because missions should flow from the vision and structure of a healthy church. As a church organizes itself around its vision, how it sees itself involved in the sowing of the gospel in the world tends to surface. A healthy Missions System expresses how your church is engaged in the larger Kingdom work both locally and around the world.

This is one of the counter-intuitive areas of increasing capacity. Sending out people and giving finances away to sow the gospel in other places—a new church a couple of miles away or reaching people in another language and land—may not seem to help you grow the church. But when your church chooses to involve itself in God's Kingdom work in the world, people are drawn and retained. This is the third system through which attenders connect deeply to your church in healthy ways.

The focus of this system is to bring thought and strategic planning to your missions approach.

To develop this system properly, you have to challenge a cultural bias that often shapes a church's mission approach. The North American church has, for several centuries, seen its role as the mission sending agency of the world, a role that has brought the gospel to many people groups. In short, they have done a good job in being witnesses to the uttermost parts of the world. Furthermore, healthy local churches have been reasonably investing in reaching their community with the gospel, their Jerusalem. Many churches are glad to participate in such mission undertakings.

Yet until recent times, the church has neglected what Jesus termed Judea and Samaria. These two represent reaching people within a region who are like us, and not like us, with the gospel. In our world, these two groups still exist, people in our state who come from the same cultural background as we have and people who are from a different people group from ours. To meet this biblical standard, your church would need to be involved in regional church planting as well as foreign and local missions.

As a result of this neglect, North America has been losing ground in reaching the nation. Although agencies and movements do exist to plant more churches, your challenge is to lead your church to actively participate in this aspect of Acts 1:8. This will involve both making church planting part of your budget and seeking to develop a daughter church strategy. Doing this will not only increase your church's capacity. It will change how you see the world in terms of the gospel—you will come to see that you live in one of the largest mission fields in the world.

Critical Questions This System Answers:

- How are we teaching attenders to have a Kingdom outlook about their lives rather than merely a personal church focus?
- Are we engaged in all three areas of mission?

Major Components:

Theology of Missions: A clarifying statement of your Missiology that will guide the development of your Missions System.

Training in Kingdom Outlook: A plan to train the congregation to develop a Kingdom outlook, seeing themselves as agents of God's Kingdom.

Financial Support: Guidelines for the church's stewardship towards missions.

Daughter Church: A strategy for starting a daughter church.

Visibility: The approach that the leaders will use to increase the visibility of missions in the church.

Coordinator: Recruiting tool for finding the person who oversees this system and helps build the missions team.

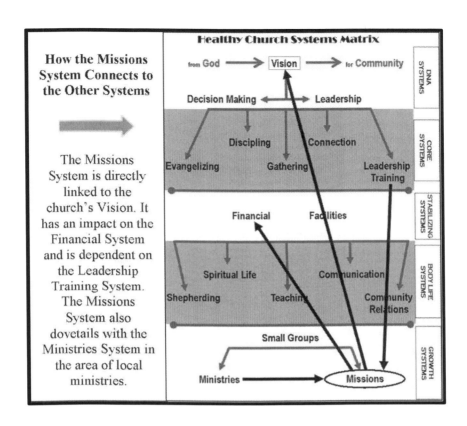

How the Missions System Connects to the Other Systems

The Missions System is directly linked to the church's Vision. It has an impact on the Financial System and is dependent on the Leadership Training System. The Missions System also dovetails with the Ministries System in the area of local ministries.

MISSIONS SYSTEM SURVEY QUESTIONS

Acts 1:8 Focus (local, regional, worldwide)

1 _____   100% of our mission support is invested in only one of the three Acts 1:8 areas.

2 _____   While our mission support is invested in two of the three Acts 1:8 areas, over 80% goes to one area.

3 _____   While our mission support is invested in all three Acts 1:8 areas, 90% of our mission support is invested in two of the three Acts 1:8 areas.

4 _____   While our mission support is invested in all three Acts 1:8 areas, over 80% goes to two areas.

5 _____   Our mission support is proportionally (not evenly) divided among the three Acts 1:8 areas, so that no two areas equal 75% of the missions budget.

Support Level

1 _____   No money is designated in the budget for missions, although individuals do give to specific missions through the church.

2 _____   Less than 5% of the budget is designated for missions. This does not include what individuals give to specific missions through the church.

3 _____   10% of the budget is designated for missions. This does not include what individuals give to specific missions through the church.

4 _____   The church has a yearly missions faith giving challenge that allows us to give more than 10% to missions.

5 _____   The church has increased its commitment to missions to over 20% of the budget.

Personal Involvement

1 _____   None of our members have ever participated in a short term mission project within the last three years.

2 _____   Church members have participated in short term missions in the last three years with another church or agency.

3 _____   Church members have participated in short term missions in the last three years that was arranged by leaders in our church.

4 _____   Our church has a short term mission focus that church members participate in yearly.

5 _____   The church is training and sending missionaries out from our congregation.

Daughter Church

1 _____   The church has no plans for starting a daughter church in the next five years.

2 _____   The church leaders have a plan for starting a daughter church in the next five years, but no money has been set aside for this and/or a potential planter has not been recruited.

3 _____   The church leaders have a plan for starting a daughter church in the next five years, with money which has been set aside for the new church. An active search is underway to identify a potential planter.

4 _____   The church has started a daughter church.

5 _____   The church has started one or more daughter churches and is planning the next one.

Leader

1 _____   Either the pastor or his wife coordinates this system or no one is assigned to oversee it.

2 _____   An untrained volunteer oversees this system.

3 _____   A trained leader over volunteers oversees this system.

4 _____   A dedicated leader leads other leaders and a team in overseeing this system.

5 _____   A dedicated leader mentoring his or her replacement and a team oversees this system.

Total _____ divided by 5 = _____

6. WHERE TO GO FROM HERE IN BUILDING SYSTEMS

Perhaps you are wondering where to go from here. If you are planting a new church, you will want to start at the beginning. The first system to address is the Vision of the church. Go from there until you have finished developing all eighteen systems. This allows you to relate your systems to the unique vision God has given you for the church. Keep referring back to your Vision as you shape each system, so that all of them help you accomplish this Vision.

As a pastor, you may not be the one who does the actual building of your church's systems, but you must value them and see that they are put into place. If you do not have the ability to develop systems (and this is common, as many pastors are big picture, not detail people) accept your limitations. Utilize team members or recruit new leaders to help you. Or hire a staff person whose main work is to build and maintain the church's systems. Also, you will find that this process will work best for your church with someone objectively coaching your team and holding them accountable.

You may want to consider a more focused approach. While working with churches that have stopped growing, I have noticed that almost all of them have five specific systems that are distressed. Not that these are the only systems they need to address. Nor is this a size issue. I have seen these same five in large as well as small churches, which is a reminder that growth is not dependent on systems alone, but on the work of God through His people. Yet leaders from churches of all sizes call on people like me because they are not satisfied that their church is healthy and sustainable over the long haul. And generally, when I evaluate the church's systems, most or all of these five show up as distressed.

Here are the five that you will want to evaluate in your church to see if they might be at the root of why your church is stuck. These five are listed in my order of concern, because the first leads to the second, the second to the third and so on. In other words, these five are symbiotic in nature (which is always the way of an organized organism). Addressing these five systems first can clear up a lot of issues for the church and lead to a greater sowing and reaping of the gospel.

1) **Neglected Spiritual Life:** This should be a huge concern for churches, but the spiritual life system is often the most underdeveloped of the eighteen. Some churches tend to believe that if prayer and Bible study are going on, the church is spiritual. In other churches, if attenders participate in certain spiritual disciplines— fasting, solitude or confession—all is well. This is not necessarily true. Many

congregations pride themselves on their spirituality and are still relatively an unhealthy group, even though they do not know it. Attenders may lack compassion, fail to be generous, be judgmental, materialistic, or compartmentalize their faith. Their faith life may be tied to the church building but not found in their home, on the road or at the workplace. This spiritual disconnect indisputably will affect all aspects of the church's health and can lead to the church being full of people who lack the inner desire to know God intimately and enjoy Him forever. This will eventually kill the future of the church and drive away the next generation, who see the poverty of such faith, and reject it. No matter what stage your church is in, this system needs to be explored first, because when you lack intimacy with God, you probably also lack a clear vision for why He has your church in your community.

2) Lack of Clear Vision: Most leaders have been schooled in the business model for vision. Vision to them is the product—what kind of church do we want to be? But after the statement is written, it can become part of the forgotten lore of the church. I have seen leadership teams of large churches that cannot remember the wording of their church's vision. But this is not the real problem. The core definition of vision for them has been altered from biblical to business. This lack of a biblical understanding of vision often drives the church to see itself as a business, offering a product that they are hoping and praying people will want. Lacking a clear biblical vision, which starts with seeing the people Jesus wants the church to have compassion for, will cause the church to fail to see the harvest they exist to gather and have no plan to gather. This lack of vision clarity lays the foundation for inconsistent evangelizing. Why? Because many churches operate in the unconscious expectation that people will come to them, instead of engaging in preparing people to go and find those for whom they are to have compassion.

3) Inconsistent Evangelizing: I know many churches wish they experienced more conversion growth. But for most really have no consistent evangelizing system. They make stabs at it, bringing in some of the best training models. In time, however, their best efforts fall by the wayside and growth again becomes dependent on 'already' believers walking through their doors and staying. Often what is wrong is not the church's desire for evangelizing, but the piecemeal approach it has taken to building this system. When I evaluate churches lacking conversion growth, what is consistently missing is evangelism accountability, which is about making evangelizing important. And so people stop evangelizing because they get busy with other ministries and causes.

4) Undefined Discipleship Process: A lack of new believers often camouflages the lack of a clear discipleship process. Yet the lack of thinking this system through is widespread. Most churches do not know that they should have a way to train new believers to follow Jesus. Nothing weakens a church more than having people who are perpetual spiritual babies. Beside this, fewer and fewer people emerge as leadership trainees, further weakening the work of the church. And in churches that do not have a discipleship process, the lack of believers growing in their faith to train as potential leaders can lead to placing immature 'warm bodies' over ministries critical to the health of the church.

5) No Leadership Training: I find that many churches do not have a plan to develop even a small pool of potential leaders. This is one of those get-to-it items on the 'to do' list of the church that never happens. Or else the church has been happily using the influx of 'already' leaders who came through their doors, ready to be put to work. So the system never becomes a priority until it is very late in the game and the need to launch more growth systems (small groups, ministries, missions) in order to connect more people to the congregation is at a critical stage. At this point, the current leaders are facing burnout due to the lack of a bench of potential leaders, which is an additional threat to the health of the church.

As you start developing and implementing necessary systems for your church, keep these five in mind. Addressing them will definitely change the life of your church.

Next Step

For step-by-step training that will strengthen your church systems and allow you to retain more disciples, go to www.ChurchEquippers.com/systems to take the next step in developing your systems. There you can get the complete *The Increasing Church Capacity Guidebook: Designing & Linking the 18 Systems* which will lead you through the process with instructions and assessment forms. Or, a Church Systems Coach can lead you through this process of strengthening your church systems.

APPENDIX 1: MEASURING YOUR SYSTEMS' HEALTH

All systems can be measured for effectiveness. The purpose of measuring is to determine if the system is actually doing what it is supposed to do. If you intend to discover the state of affairs with your current systems, you will need to measure them quantitatively. Quantitative measurement assumes that all systems produce something that can be counted in some way. This helps you to avoid the anecdotal evaluation approach. Anecdotal evaluation looks at the history of the system rather than its current state. It prevents leaders from realizing something is a hindrance to the healthy growth of the church because sometime in the past, the system was productive. Times change and although a system was effective in the past it may no longer impact the disciples you have or are trying to reach with the gospel.

Besides a quantitative measurement, all church systems can be summarized with a qualitative measurement, which is called the 'necessary outcome.' You will find these at the top of each system module. As you evaluate your church's systems, the qualitative measurement will either be true or not true. There is no middle ground if you are honestly seeking to strengthen the work of your church or build the foundational systems for a new church plant.

In system thinking, the necessary outcome is the label for the proper product of the system. All the various parts of the systems flow together to produce this outcome. When the necessary outcome is being produced at its maximum strength, it flows together with the other 17 systems to produce healthy growth in the church, as shown below.

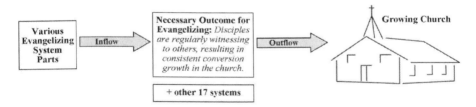

However, if the church is not growing, this is a sign that the necessary outcomes for one or more systems are not being reached. When that is true, this creates a feedback loop, which is a signal to reexamine the system's parts to see if they are both working properly and contributing.

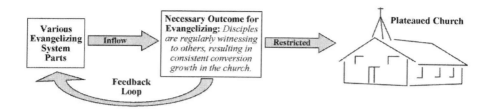

The feedback loops means that you will need to go back and determine if you will need to rebuild some or all of that system's parts. In the case of an evangelizing system, are people engaged in prayer for the lost? Are they being trained properly to be witnesses? Is there ongoing accountability? Do the whole church strategies fit the people we are seeking to reach with the gospel? A rigorous examination is what called for when the necessary outcome is not being produced by the system.

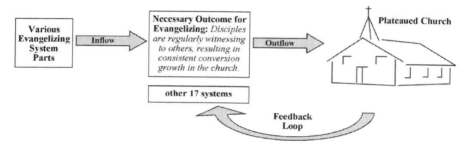

You will need to practice discernment however. The feedback loop may be pointing to a broken upline issue. Perhaps there is nothing wrong with your evangelizing system. Through it, people regularly are saying 'yes' to Jesus, but they are not staying in the church, thus not producing consistent conversion growth. This problem is then producing a different feedback loop, not from the necessary outcome to your evangelizing system, but from the church to one or more of the other systems.

A feedback loop signals that you need to revisit the health of one or more of your systems. But it is to your advantage to do a regular quantitative check up on your systems before your church becomes plateaued.

APPENDIX 2: CONNECTING SYSTEMS TO NATURAL CHURCH DEVELOPMENT

You may choose to use the Natural Church Development survey to discern what your church needs to address. The NCD offers eight characteristics of a healthy church. The survey reveals what is called the "minimum factor"—the one characteristic that is causing your church not to retain attenders and grow. Below are the eight NCD characteristics with a description of what each addresses. Included are also the corresponding systems of the eighteen in this manual that need to tweaked in light of your minimum factor. *(Information on taking an NCD survey can be obtained through Church Smart Resources at www.churchsmart.com.)*

Empowering Leaders: Covers the issues of: 1) Spiritual Empowerment of the Leader; 2) Leaders empower others; 3) Leadership fit; 4) Delegation and sharing of ministry; and 5) Compelling vision.

- ❖ System 1: Vision

- ❖ System 2: Leadership

- ❖ System 3: Decision Making

- ❖ System 8: Leadership Training

- ❖ System 12: Spiritual Life

Gift-Oriented Ministry: Covers the issues of: 1) Integrating gifts into ministry flow; 2) Significance of ministry; 3) Support for ministry; and 4) Equipping for ministry.

- ❖ System 17: Ministries

- ❖ System 18: Missions

Passionate Spirituality: Covers the issues of: 1) Experiencing God; 2) Passion for church; 3) Passion for devotions; and 4) Spiritual interconnectedness.

- ❖ System 12: Spiritual Life

- ❖ System 13: Teaching

Effective Structures: Covers the issues of: 1) Effective planning; 2) Organizational structures and systems; 3) Innovation and managing change; and 4) Structure for effective leadership.

- ❖ System 5: Discipling

- ❖ System 7: Connection

- ❖ System 8: Leadership Training

- ❖ System 9: Financial

- ❖ System 10: Facilities

- ❖ System 14: Communication

Inspiring Worship: Covers the issues of: 1) Personal transformation in worship; 2) Visitor friendly church; 3) Relevancy of preaching; 4) Anticipation for worship; and 5) Care for children.

- ❖ System 6: Gathering

- ❖ System 7: Connection

- ❖ System 12: Spiritual Life

Holistic Small Groups: Covers the issues of: 1) Developing spiritually-oriented communities; 2) Multiplication of disciples, leaders, and groups; 3) Integrating newcomers; and 4) Group relevance.

- ❖ System 5: Discipling

- ❖ System 8: Leadership Training

- ❖ System 12: Spiritual Life

- ❖ System 16: Small Groups

Need-Oriented Evangelism: Covers the issues of: 1) Friendly church; 2) Corporate evangelistic efforts; 3) Personal evangelism; and 4) Seeker-sensitive church.

- ❖ System 4: Evangelizing

- ❖ System 6: Gathering

- ❖ System 7: Connection

- ❖ System 12: Spiritual Life

- ❖ System 15: Community Relations

Loving Relationships: Covers the issues of: 1) Atmosphere of joy and trust; 2) Interdependent relationships; 3) Affirmation and encouragement; and 4) Intentional conflict resolution.

- ❖ System 7: Connection

- ❖ System 11: Shepherding

- ❖ System 12: Spiritual Life

SPECIAL OFFER

Go to www.ChurchEquippers.com/iccpromo to schedule a

Free 30 min. Systems Consultation

LIMITED AVAILABILITY - OFFER EXPIRES 12/31/14

For additional material on church systems go to
www.ChurchEquippers.com/systems

Other books by Dr. Steve Smith
Available at ChurchEquippers.com/books

For additional tools, please visit:

www.ChurchEquippers.com